H. Martyn Kennard

Philistines and Israelites

A New Light on the World's History

H. Martyn Kennard

Philistines and Israelites
A New Light on the World's History

ISBN/EAN: 9783744734004

Printed in Europe, USA, Canada, Australia, Japan

Cover: Foto ©ninafisch / pixelio.de

More available books at **www.hansebooks.com**

PHILISTINES AND ISRAELITES

A NEW LIGHT ON THE WORLD'S HISTORY

BY

H. MARTYN KENNARD

LONDON: CHAPMAN & HALL, L^{D.}
1893.

PHILISTINES & ISRAELITES

A New Light on the World's History.

CHAPTER I.

"Errors, to be dangerous, must have a great deal of truth mingled with them; it is only from this alliance that they can ever obtain an extensive circulation: from pure extravagance, and genuine, unmingled falsehood, the world never has and never can sustain any mischief."

Sydney Smith.

THE Philistines and the Israelites have been stamped on our thoughts from earliest infancy; few have cared to investigate their origin; thus any new light thrown on their history will be interesting to many.

We learn from the Biblical records that the three races of Shem, Ham, and Japheth dominated the world; it follows that the Philistines and the Israelites must have belonged to one or the other of these three families. I shall endeavour to point out that, in the Biblical narratives, the Philistines represent the Hamitic race, and the Israelites personate the race of Shem.

The reader must be warned that the problem requires to be followed as closely as a proposition in Euclid, for my task is a very perplexing one.

M. Renan pointedly observes:—"It has never been established by observation that a superior being troubles himself, for a moral or immoral purpose, with the things of nature or the affairs of mankind." I need not point out that such a conception shatters the very foundation stone of the Biblical narratives. We may, therefore, dismiss from our minds all supernatural agencies as factors in the guidance of mankind and follow the dictates of reason in our historical research.

I approach my subject with profound diffidence, for the views I shall advance will clash with those of our greatest scholars. I can only hope that my very startling suggestions may receive fair consideration.

Professor Sayce, in his very interesting

Ernest Renan, "History of the People of Israel," Preface, xi., Second Division.

Philistines and Israelites.

little work on "A Forgotten Empire," gives us a map illustrating the extent of this ancient empire. It covers a country from the Euxine in the north to Egypt in the south, from the Tigris in the east to the Mediterranean in the west.

Although this Hittite Empire probably existed in remote times, I venture to suggest that it cannot be the Hittite Empire of the Old Testament; Biblical historians apparently knew nothing of it; it had become lost to view through conquests, and we may reasonably conjecture that long before the time of Chedorlaomer, the Elamites had subjugated these Hittites and secured dominion from Elam to Thebes.

Genesis xiv.

We must first understand that the fellaheen, whom we may regard as the indigenous population of Egypt, have always been a subject race; this goes to the root of the whole argument, for it is manifest that the priestly writers would have us believe that the fellaheen have represented, through all Egyptian history, the power of Egypt; whereas, in reality, they never had a voice in any Egyptian Government which has

Philistines and Israelites.

existed since the time of the Elamite Pharaoh Menes.

I shall point out that the Hamitic and Semitic races alternately dominated the entire eastern Empire; hence the indigenous populations in every province must have ranked themselves under the two dominant flags.

Before I proceed I must beg the reader to bear in mind that peoples have acquired their names from the territorial divisions they occupy; unless this is understood we shall lose sight of racial distinctions; for instance, when the Normans conquered and occupied England they soon became known as Englishmen; consequently the Norman race has become almost lost to view; and so it was when the Elamites conquered and occupied the Hittite country, their race became obscured through acquiring the names of the various territorial divisions in which they settled.

It stands to reason that when the Elamites occupied the Hittite country they became known as Hittites, thus there were two distinct Hittite races on the scene, viz., the subjugated Hittites and their conquerors, who acquired the name of Hittites. The monuments and inscriptions clearly point this out, and Professor Sayce tells us that the ancient Hittites were of a totally different race from the Hittites of the Old Testament.

The Hittites, and E. 15.

I need not point out that this view has a general application. Races, then, can only be traced by their flags; during revolutions these flags became conspicuous, so we can readily follow them.

It is true we have heard very little about the Elamites; their history has been adroitly obscured by the priestly writers.

It is however well known, that the so-called Chaldeans exercised supreme influence in the East; and, as we may be certain, that the Elamites occupied Chaldea before the invasion of Abraham, we can only conclude that the people known at this period as Chaldeans were Elamites.

The reader will detect, as we proceed, that the method adopted by historians in alluding to races by the name of the

Philistines and Israelites.

territorial division they happen at the moment to occupy leads to great confusion, and has almost obscured true history.

It has been palpably the aim of the priestly writers to obscure races; for a God-protected people termed Hebrews are placed dimly on the scene, and upon them is centred their historical review. I shall, however, point out that they were only a combination in the priestly plot, and serve, in the Biblical design, as a link to confuse and blend together the two great rival races. We shall find that Abraham the Cushite and Joseph the Elamite are both alluded to as Hebrews. The object is obvious; for it was necessary, in order to frame a claim of Divine Right to universal dominion, that the two paramount races should be blended into one.

The celebrated list of the Pharaoh Seti's ancestors discloses that all the Pharaohs down to the fall of the XIIth Egyptian dynasty were of one race; and as Seti passes over all the Pharaohs of the XIIIth to the close of the XVIIth dynasty, we can only conclude that these Pharaohs were of

Genesis xiv. 13; xxxix. 14.

See Nile Gleanings, Villiers Stuart, 323.

a different race. The inscriptions unmistakably confirm this.

A mighty revolution then must have occurred on the close of the XIIth dynasty, and as Seti claims as his ancestors the Pharaohs of the XVIIIth dynasty, it becomes apparent that his family was kept out of power, owing to this revolution, for some seven centuries.

We have, then, one single race in power for some two or three thousand years, displaced by another race which holds dominion for seven hundred years; consequently we have only two races before us competing for supremacy; I must contend that every possible device has been adopted to obscure these two races; but, as we may assure ourselves that the Biblical narratives, although garbled and distorted to further the interests of priestcraft, are based upon authentic records, we have only to read between the lines and the two great races are distinctly exposed.

When we turn to Genesis we find it recorded that Abraham, advancing from the East, defeated the Great Elamite King

Genesis xiv.

Chedorlaomer, which secured him a dominion extending from the Euphrates to Egypt. This is the territory known as the Promised land. The reader will notice that if the Almighty presented this territory to the Cushites it was at the expense of the Elamites, which would account for the deadly hatred existing between the two races; and, as the promise was only given to the race of Abraham, the motive for blending the two races together is very distinctly indicated.

Dates are certainly problematical in such remote times, for the simple reason that history has been distorted. There cannot, however, arise any confusion in our minds as to the identity of a revolution which supplanted a dynasty which had ruled for thousands of years, and left them in subjection for seven centuries; thus when we find it recorded that Abraham invaded Western Asia and conquered the Elamites under their Great King Chedorlaomer, we may be morally certain that this revolution synchronizes with the fall of the XIIth Egyptian dynasty; and further, that the XIIth dynasty represented the Elamite power.

Genesis xv. 18.

Philistines and Israelites.

Here then, we have the Semitic race disclosed; for we have it recorded that Elam was the eldest son of Shem. *Genesis x. 22.*

The race led by Abraham has certainly been very carefully obscured; it was vital to the priestly design that it should be concealed, but now that we have discovered the great race which must have exercised sovereignty over the Eastern Empire extending from Elam to Thebes for thousands of years, does it not glaringly reveal the ingenuity of historians in concealing the race which vanquished them; but as the priestly narratives are based upon authentic records, we can, by the aid of inscriptions which have escaped destruction, still fathom the mystery. Let us turn to their early revelation of the world's history and we find it recorded that there were three great families represented by Shem, Ham, and Japheth. Abraham certainly recalls Father Ham, and as we learn that his eldest son was Cush, may we not conclude that Abraham represented the Cushite or Hamitic race. It is no rash conjecture, for I shall point out that the descendants of the royal *Genesis x. 6.*

family of Abraham all styled themselves kings, or kings sons of Cush.

Here, then, we have the other great competing race very clearly defined.

Now that we have discovered the two great races, I shall follow their fortunes under their racial designations of Elamites and Cushites. They are designedly presented to us in the Biblical narratives under many territorial and fanciful appellations; consequently their racial distinctions have been almost lost to view.

The reader must understand, if he wishes to follow me, that the two races became blended together and permeated every province within the Eastern Empire; they cannot, therefore, be localised as separate nations; and, as the two royal families became united by marriage in blood relationship, we can only hope to follow them by their respective flags.

Genesis xiv. We gather from the records that the Cushite Abraham overthrew the power of Elam and acquired dominion over the entire Eastern Empire; for, if we read between the lines, he is distinctly disclosed in Egypt.

Philistines and Israelites.

The priestly historian Flavius Josephus gives us some remarkable information, said to be extracted from Manetho, a learned Egyptian priest, who is supposed to have written a history of his country about 280 B.C. He informs us that a wild and rude people of inglorious origin, from the region of the East, suddenly swooped down on Egypt, conquered the native kings who dwelt there, and took possession of the whole country, without meeting any great opposition on the part of the Egyptians. This singular notice of such a mighty revolution is abruptly capped by the statement, "The whole people bore the name of Hyksos," and, as we might anticipate, this has been reiterated by all historians; but as it is well known that these would-be "unknown people of inglorious origin" continued to occupy Egypt for some seven centuries; such a statement is palpably absurd and repugnant to reason.

I must submit it is absolutely impossible that an undisciplined horde, coming from no one knew where, could have wrested the power of Egypt out of the hands of the greatest nation in the world, and have held it for seven hundred years, without their history being very well known to every early historian. It is glaringly apparent that no power could have crossed the Euphrates and occupied Egypt before crushing the power of Elam, therefore such a conquest is inconsistent with common sense. But if we understand that it was vital to a priestly design, that Abraham should be stripped of his worldly power, and appear before us as a simple shepherd under the personal guidance and protection of the Almighty, then we shall recognise that this version of the Hyksos occupation of Egypt is a tale, adroitly distorted, for the purpose of obscuring true history. It is based upon a substratum of truth which makes it so dangerous; for inscriptions tell us that a change of dynasty did occur in Egypt at this period; we may, therefore, be absolutely certain that the Hyksos must represent the Cushites, who succeeded in subduing the Elamites, and acquired dominion over the whole Empire. Abraham beyond a doubt was not a wandering shep-

Philistines and Israelites.

herd, but the chief of the mighty Cushite nation. I must leave it to students to say under which name we may recognise him in the royal lists. I am well aware it is conjectured that these so-called Hyksos did not invade Egypt for some centuries after the fall of the XIIth dynasty—but as we know that the XIIth dynasty did fall about 2,200 B.C., we have to find the race which could have overthrown the greatest power in the world; and when we have it recorded that Abraham did overthrow the Elamites under Chedorlaomer about 2,200 B.C., we are actually forced to the conclusion that Abraham, that is father Ham, who certainly represents the Hamitic race, did subjugate the race of Shem (Elamites) represented by Chedorlaomer. We may also reasonably conjecture that the Hamitic race may have effected their conquest of Egypt through Nubia. We certainly find the symbol Nub associated with the Hyksos kings, which recalls Nubia. We also learn from the inscriptions that the Pharaoh Hirhor styled himself as King's Son of Cush, and Cush again recalls Nubia.

Philistines and Israelites.

This is strongly confirmed, for we find that nearly all the expeditions of the XIIth dynasty were directed against the Ethiopians who clearly represent the Nubians or Cushites; hence we might suppose that the so-called Hyksos' conquest of Nubia preceded their conquest of Egypt and Western Asia. Thus the XIIIth and XIVth dynasties would represent an unsettled government as indicated in the inscriptions. Again we find it recorded by Manetho that the so-called Hyksos occupied Memphis and especially fortified the Eastern frontiers, for they foresaw that the Assyrians, who were then the most powerful people, would endeavour to make an attack on their kingdom.

Brugsch, vol. i. 262. Translation by Phillip Smith, 2nd edition.

This is very important, for we find it recorded that Asshur, who undoubtedly personates the Assyrians, was the son of Elam, the son of Shem.

Genesis x. 22.

We are therefore irresistibly led to the conclusion that the so-called Hyksos were the Hamitic Cushites, and their rivals were the Semitic Elamites.

We must now understand that the

Philistines and Israelites.

Cushites had subjugated the Elamites, and gained possession of Egypt. This occupation is shadowed in the Biblical narratives.

As this great revolution has been ascribed by historians to the Hyksos, and the term so pervades all Egyptian history of this period, I must, for the sake of avoiding confusion, occasionally refer to the Cushites as the Hyksos. It has been ascertained that they acquired dominion in Egypt about 2200 B.C., and continued to occupy it for some seven centuries, their rule is a very obscure one and I need not dwell upon it; but we find them dislodged from power about 1500 B.C. I must contend that there is no other race known to us which could have effected such a momentous revolution but the Elamites. During the seven hundred years of Hyksos rule they had gradually crept into power. This may be traced in the Biblical narratives in Joseph's accession to high distinction; and we may be certain that Aahmes, the Pharaoh who deposed Apepi the last Pharaoh of the Hyksos dynasty, was none other than Joseph.

Genesis xii. 10.

Ragozin, Story of the Nations, Chaldea, 224.

Philistines and Israelites.

We learn from the inscriptions that Aahmes, who founded the XVIIIth dynasty, expelled the Hyksos from Thebes; they however still continued their hold on the Delta during forty years, to which we may dimly trace the forty years wandering, and were finally driven from Egypt about 1500 B.C., under their Pharaoh Apepi.

I have pointed out that no other race but the Elamites could have effected such a revolution; this is abundantly confirmed, for Aahmes, who secured the throne of Egypt, is claimed by Seti as his ancestor. This must convince us that the Pharaohs of the XIIth dynasty were of the same race as the Pharaohs of the XVIIIth dynasty.

During their long rule the Cushites in Egypt would certainly have acquired the territorial name of Egyptians; they may also have been termed Hyksos and were probably known under many other appellations; but I must impress on the reader that none of these names give us any indication of their nationality.

If we are to believe the tale, handed down by Josephus, that they were a race

Philistines and Israelites.

of inglorious origin coming from no one knows where, then we must understand, when they were expelled from Egypt, they retreated, no one knows whither, for they appear to vanish from the scene; and not alone Egypt but the world knows them no more; and yet previous to their retreat, for a space of some seven hundred years, they were the greatest nation in the world.

He who runs may read, provided he can read; and, the records plainly tell us, that they were still a mighty people; but as we know there were only two great nations struggling for supremacy in the Eastern Empire, these two rival powers stand out prominently on the scene as the Elamites and the Cushites. When, therefore, the Cushite forces were expelled from Egypt, may we not be certain that they only retreated to their dominions in Asia, where, as the inscriptions inform us, they were very shortly after attacked by the Elamites forces under Joshua. (*i.e.* Joseph.) (*i.e.* Aahmes.)

In the great catalogue of the towns of

Philistines and Israelites.

Brugsch's Egypt, vol. i. 269.

Western Asia conquered by Thotmes III., whose inhabitants submitted to the Egyptian rule after the battle of Megiddo, they are described as all the population of the upper land of Rutennu; and Brugsch adds: "This proves in the most positive manner that the name of Upper Rutennu must have coincided almost exactly with the country included later within the boundaries of the twelve tribes of Israel." But does it not also indicate that neither the territorial division of Israel, or the Israelities, were known at this period; it therefore becomes apparent that the revolution we are discussing was a conflict for supremacy in the empire between the Cushites and the Elamites; so we must understand that the Elamites are now again supreme from Elam to Thebes, and the Cushites are in the cold shade of opposition under the house of Apepi the deposed Cushite Pharaoh of the XVIIth Egyptian dynasty. We may, however, be morally certain that they still held dominion in Ethiopia.

We will now turn to the retreat of the

Hyksos from Egypt. It has been ascertained, from the monuments and other authentic sources, that they were dislodged from Thebes during the XVIIth Egyptian dynasty, and Joseph (*i.e.*, Aahmes) their conqueror founded the XVIIIth dynasty. It has also been discovered that Apepi was their king at the time of their retreat, and their forces were finally expelled from the Delta about 1500 B.C.

We gather from Bunsen that during the first century A.D. a controversy took place between two celebrated scholars as to the origin of the Jews. Apion contended that the exodus under Moses was nothing else but a revolt of leprous outcasts, who, at a much later period, established themselves under an apostate priest, Osarsiph, of Heliopolis, in the ancient Hyksos city (of Tanis), which had been made over to them, and then called to their aid the old enemies of the Empire. Josephus, in answer, asserts that "the Jews are the old lords of Egypt, who, after many centuries of glorious dominion, at length quitted it under an honourable convention and the guidance of

Bunsen's Egypt. vol. i. 193, 1848.

Moses, *long before* the supposed date of that fabulous story." This view of the great scholar, Josephus, respecting the origin of the Jews, must convince us that he was not the Jewish historian known as Flavius Josephus. It would also indicate that these great scholars were unacquainted with the Books of Moses in their present form.

See Edwin Johnson's Rise of Christendom, Introduction, '5.

The late Cardinal Newman tells us that " all knowledge of the Latin classics comes to us from the mediæval copies of them, and they who transcribed them had an opportunity of forging or garbling them. We are simply at their mercy. . . . The existing copies, whenever made, are to us the autographic originals." Can it be doubted that the priestly writers would forge, garble or destroy every shred of evidence inconsistent with their design?

We have the forgers' den graphically described by one behind the scenes, for Father Hardouin presents us to the rogues sitting down in their *scriptoria*, with sixth, seventh, eighth, ninth or tenth century ink and parchments, with corresponding alphabets, to write works in the names of

Philistines and Israelites.

imaginary authors. He designates the producers of the first Church literature as "a wicked and impious crew of Atheists, whose virus had infected the Missal even, and the Breviary."

<small>*Father Hardouin, Ad Censuram Veterum Scriptorum Prolegomena (1766).*</small>

It is apparent that pure romance could never have been accepted as trustworthy history, we must therefore understand that the Biblical narratives are invariably based upon authentic records, but they have been so adroitly distorted that the truth absolutely conceals the truth; if, however, we follow them carefully the distortions may easily be detected, and if we eliminate them true history will be revealed.

I must again impress upon the reader that the people inhabiting territorial divisions, whether great or small, acquire their name from the division in which they reside; and unless we recognise that these territorial names give no indication of race we shall lose touch of the political situation.

I have pointed out that the forces of the so-called Hyksos were expelled from Egypt under their Pharaoh Apepi by Aahmes, who founded the XVIIIth Egyptian dynasty;

Philistines and Israelites.

we may be absolutely certain that these Hyksos, through their occupation of Egypt during a period of seven centuries, had acquired the name of Egyptians; and we may be equally sure that when they quitted Egypt they would become known by another name; and, as we apparently lose sight of them in the Biblical records, let us endeavour to trace them; and we must bear in mind that during their dominion in Egypt, and probably Western Asia, they were the greatest nation in the world. Dates may be problematical, but we may assure ourselves that the fall of this mighty power occurred some time about 1500 B.C. It will be admitted such a revolution was a singular and momentous one, and it is not at all probable that any other similar event of such magnitude could have clashed with it, so as to create confusion in our minds in identifying it; when, therefore, we gather from the Biblical records that a great exodus took place from Egypt about this period, we should be forced to conclude that this exodus must refer to the retreat of the Hyksos; but, if this is denied, dates

Philistines and Israelites.

become all important. I presume it will be admitted that the Biblical exodus refers to the retreat of a special and single race from Egypt into Palestine. It has been ascertained that the Temple in Jerusalem was founded by the Jews in 1017 B.C., and, as it is recorded that this event took place 480 years after their retreat from Egypt, we can date their retreat to 1497 B.C.; so here we have a fixed date for the retreat of the Jews from Egypt; and, as I have pointed out that the retreat of the Hyksos is supposed to have taken place about this period, may we not with certainty conclude that the Biblical Jewish exodus is identical with the Hyksos retreat?[1. Kings, vi. 1.]

I must beg the reader to understand that this is no new theory; for the learned scholar Josephus (not the spurious Flavius Josephus) asserts: "that the Jews are the old lords of Egypt, who, after many centuries of glorious dominion, at length quitted it under an honourable convention, and the guidance of Moses;" and Bunsen himself adds: "In our judgment there is no better grounded hypothesis than that of the affinity [Bunsen Egypt, vol. i. 19.] [Ibid] of race between the Hyksos and the Jews." Hence, when we find that Apepi, the last king of the Egyptian XVIIth dynasty, did lead the Hyksos out of Egypt at the precise date given by the Biblical writers as the date of the Jewish exodus, we are forced to the conclusion that Moses and Apepi are identical personages.

I. Kings iv. 1.

Again we learn from Strabo, speaking of Judea: "Most of the country is said to be inhabited by mixed tribes of Egyptians, Arabians, and Phœnicians, there being such a mixture of population, the prevailing report of those connected with the Temple in Jerusalem, say that: 'The ancestors of those now called Jews were Egyptians.'" Here, then, again we have massive evidence that the Jews were formerly known as Egyptians, and were the descendants of the Hyksos.

I have suggested that the so-called Hyksos would undoubtedly have acquired the name of Egyptians, owing to their residence in the territorial division of Egypt, and soon after they had retreated from Egypt they would certainly have acquired

Philistines and Israelites.

the territorial name of the divisions they settled in; but I must again remind the reader that the so-called Hyksos were Cushites, and the race which had expelled them from Egypt were Elamites, and we must understand that these two races were the greatest powers in the world. I will therefore venture to assert that the forces led by Apepi (*i.e.* Moses), when they evacuated Egypt, may not have been greatly exaggerated in the Biblical narratives. It is true that the Cushites had been defeated in Egypt, but it is more than probable that they were still masters of all the fortresses in Western Asia; and I must again repeat, if the reader wishes to follow me, he must understand this, and recognise that Moses represents Apepi, the deposed Pharaoh of the XVIIth Egyptian dynasty. It may appear a very startling demand, but, as I proceed, it will very soon become apparent that confidence is justified. If, then, we understand that Moses was Apepi, we have in the distorted books of Exodus, Joshua, and Judges a garbled account of the retreat of the Cushites from Egypt.

I will now proceed to give my reasons why I conjecture that Moses was the Cushite Pharaoh. I rely on no less an authority than Professor Sayce, and give his letter to the Academy in full :

"The Name of Moses in the Cuneiform Tablets of Tel-El-Armana.

"Queen's College, Oxford : June 3, 1888.

"The cuneiform tablets discovered last winter at Tel-el-Amarna in Upper Egypt turn out to be even more interesting and important than I supposed. About 160 of them have been procured for the museum at Vienna, and have been examined there by Doctors Winchler and Lehmann. The result of their examination shows that the Amasis, whose name is found on one of M. Bouriant's tablets, does not belong to the XXVIth dynasty, as I had imagined, but to the XVIIIth, and that the tablets themselves formed part of the archives of Amenophis III. and IV. They consist, for the most part, of letters and despatches sent to these monarchs by the kings and governors of Palestine, Syria, Mesopotamia, and Babylonia; and, as some of them were written by Burna-buryas, King of Babylon, their age is about 1430 B.C. I will not say anything here upon the new vistas in Oriental history which such an extraordinary discovery opens up, since my copies and translations of the tablets belonging to M. Bouriant will appear before long in the Proceedings of the Society of Biblical Archaeology. But there is one fact brought to light by them which is so curious that I connot refrain from laying it before the readers of the *Academy*. In my Hibbert Lectures last year I pointed out that the Hebrew Mosheh or Moses is letter for letter the Assyrian Masu, and I gave reasons for believing that Masu would prove to have originally been a name of the Sun-god. One of the tablets from Tel-el-Amarna has confirmed my conclusions sooner than I expected. It contains a reference to the Sun-god rising from the divine day, whose name is Masi, or Masu. Masu was, therefore, a name already known in Egypt a hundred years before the date assigned by Egyptologists to the Exodus, and it is further proved that it was the name of the Babylonian Sun-god before it was the name of a man."

I will now refer the reader to Professor Hommel's views relating to the connection between Egypt and Babylon as reported in the *Times* of Wednesday, 7th September, 1892.

"Semitic Section.

"In the Babylonian and Assyrian subdivision of this section, of which Professor Sayce is president, Professor F. Hommel of Munich read a paper on 'The Babylonian Origin of Egyptian Culture.' After analysing the ancient Pantheon of Babylonia, and especially that of its oldest city, Eridhu, the author showed that the names of the gods corresponded in many cases with the names of deities mentioned in the oldest Egyptian pyramid texts. These identifications were not merely confined to names, for they frequently found that these names were represented by exactly the same signs in both Babylonian and Egyptian antiquities. He mentioned as the most remarkable

Philistines and Israelites.

instance the name and signs of Osiris, the Babylonian Asari, which in both Babylon and Egypt was represented by an eye and a seat. He contended that there had been a direct communication between the two civilisations, and that the Babylonian was the older of the two. He raised strong objections to the theories that had been put forward as to the Semitic origin of the Egyptian language, maintaining that the older texts clearly indicated an affinity with the Sumerian dialect of Babylonia."

We may, therefore, rest assured that the Egyptian fellaheen have ever been a subjected race ; and, as there were only two great powers struggling together for supremacy in the Empire, it follows that the Egyptian Pharaohs were either Cushites or Elamites. And the Abydus tablet, recording the ancestors of the Pharaoh Seti, will enable us to classify them.

Professor Sayce again tells us: "The letters from Palestine (Tel-el-Amarna tablets) establish the fact that reading and writing were widely known and practised in the country at the close of the fifteenth

Records of the Past (N. S.), vol. v. 64.

century before our era. But the writing was that of Babylonia, thus proving the deep impression which had been made by Babylonian culture upon Western Asia. It is difficult to account for the impression except upon the hypothesis of Babylonian conquest. The hypothesis is confirmed by the number of places in Palestine which took their name from Babylonian deities. Rimmon, the Babylonian Ramman, Anah and Anath, the Babylonian Anu and Anat, Nebo and even Sin are all found in Palestine or the countries immediately adjoining."

A foreign conquest of the country is therefore clearly indicated. But when we recognise that the Babylonians represented the Hamitic and Semitic dominant races, we may be morally certain that their two cults permeated through the length and breadth of the entire Empire, and they have been designedly obscured to further the aims of priestcraft. When therefore the flag of Elam was dominant, the Elamite worship was the State religion, and when the Cushites were in power their religion was paramount.

Philistines and Israelites.

We may be certain that there were only two great races and two prominent cults within the eastern Empire. This becomes confirmed by the Biblical writers when they disclose religious reforms after every change of government in the small provinces of Judea and Israel.

I shall point out that Apepi, the last Pharaoh of the Cushite Hyksos XVIIth dynasty, was a worshipper of the Sun God Masu, and as the Pharaohs were recognised as deities, Apepi became known as Moses, which Professor Sayce tells us is "letter for letter" the same as Masu.

CHAPTER II.

I HAVE ventured to assert that the so-called Hyksos represent the race of Abraham, consequently Apepi (*i.e* Moses), the last of the Hyksos Pharaohs of the XVIIth dynasty, was of the race of Abraham ; and, let us remember, that Seti claims none of the Hyksos Pharaohs as his ancestors, but he does claim Aahmes, who deposed Apepi. It stands to reason, then, that the Elamites had vanquished their rivals the Cushites.

We can only conclude that when the Hyksos forces retreated from Egypt a section of them occupied Canaan, and acquired the name of Philistines; and if we follow the Books of Joshua and Judges, we shall find that constant conflicts are recorded between the Philistines and Israelites. We can therefore only conclude that the Philistines and the Israelites represent the two rival races, which the priestly writers are so anxious to obscure.

Philistines and Israelites. 33

It becomes evident that when Apepi (*i.e.* Moses) led the Hyksos forces from Egypt they were a defeated race. He had resisted a formidable attack from the Elamite Pharaoh on crossing the frontier; his troops must have been sorely tried in crossing the desert, but we may conjecture he safely reached Judea, and intrenched his army in the fortresses on the sea coast. This enabled him to dominate all Canaan, which henceforth became known as Philistia, so we must understand that this section of the Hyksos became called Philistines; and, if we read between the lines of the Biblical records, we can only conclude that the Elamites under Joseph, Hoshea, or Joshua the son of Nun, succeeded in defeating Apepi (*i.e.* Moses), and regained possession of the Empire; the Philistines retiring to their strongholds on the sea coast. Hence if we recognise that the Philistines represent a section of the Hyksos, and that the Israelites represent a section of the Elamite power, it becomes vividly manifest that the struggle for supremacy in the Empire is as hotly

Exodus xiv. 9.

Zephaniah ii. 5.

Deuteronomy xxxii. 44.

contested as ever between the two great rival races.

We gather from the inscriptions that the Hyksos were not reduced to slavery, hence the retreat of the Hyksos could have had no connection with an exodus of slaves. It follows, then, that there must have been two exoduses, and probably many more; but let us bear in mind that the retreat of the Hyksos under Apepi is known to have occurred about 1500 B.C.; it has to be fitted in between the rule of the Hyksos, which occupied a period of some seven centuries, and the dynasty of Aahmes, which continued in power for two centuries, If, then, we can date the retreat of the Jews to 1500 B.C.—that is, 480 years before the building of the Temple in Jerusalem—we may be morally certain that the retreat of the Hyksos and the exodus of the Jews are identical events. It also further explains that the Jews were the descendants of the Hyksos, and this is confirmed by the scholars Josephus and Strabo.

The reader must, however, understand that as the two great races permeated every province in the empire, the inhabitants of Judea consisted of a section of both races, who would all be called Jews; hence, we must not forget that there were two distinct races of Jews in Judea, viz., the Cushite Jews and the Elamite Jews. The priestly writers have taken every advantage of this combination to confuse them together and blend them into one race. When, therefore, I refer to the retreat of the Jews from Egypt I allude only to the Cushite or Hyksos Jews.

The Elamite Pharaoh Aahmes is succeeded by seven members of his family, when we come to the reign of Khuenaten.

I have the good fortune to be associated with Professor Flinders Petrie in Egyptian research, and during the past season he has been engaged in exploring the ruins of Khuenaten's royal palace at Tel-el-Amarna. The relics brought to light not only disclose that a religious revolution had taken place, but a distinct style and an advance in art is discernable. Professor Petrie tells us that "the origin of this new departure cannot have been any national movement, or it would not have been annihilated so soon after." May we then not detect in Khuenaten's reign a revolution which brought the Cushite Hyksos into power? This is confirmed; for we find that Seti does not include Khuenaten and his dynasty in his list of ancestors, so we may be morally certain that Khuenaten was a Cushite Pharaoh. I shall point out that Khuenaten was the Pharaoh "which knew not Joseph."

The monuments discovered by Professor Petrie disclose that Khuenaten was peacefully succeeded by three members of his family, and that they were all ardent followers of the Sun God Aten, or Masu. We are therefore forced to the conclusion that Khuenaten was a lineal descendant of Abraham and Apepi, and as we find that the Tel-el-Amarna despatches to Khuenaten are entitled "To the King my Lord, my God, My Sun God who is from heaven," we may assure ourselves that Abraham and Apepi were also worshippers of the Sun God; when, therefore, Apepi retreated from Egypt he would be styled as the Sun God. This will explain how Apepi became known as

Palestine Exploration Fund, October, 1892, 293.

Philistines and Israelites.

Moses, for Professor Sayce informs us that the Sun God Masu is, letter for letter, the same as Moses. Khuenaten is succeeded by three members of his family, when another revolution is disclosed. Horemhib, who is claimed by Seti as his ancestor, now secures dominion, the royal palace of Khuenaten at Tel-el-Amarna is destroyed, and the worship of the Sun God suppressed. Horemhib is succeeded by Ramses I. and then by Seti himself, who is followed by the great warrior Ramses II. Clearly then we have the Elamite Pharaohs before us.

I must submit this proves beyond a doubt that there were only two rival races struggling together for supremacy in the Empire; their great conflicts, so clearly defined in the inscriptions, have been adroitly narrowed by the priestly writers into petty engagements between Philistines and Israelites. It therefore becomes evident that the Biblical narratives not only obscure the two great races, but the Empire in which Judea and Israel were merely ciphers.

Philistines and Israelites.

The Egyptian inscriptions here give us material assistance. Ramses II. is disclosed as constantly invading Western Asia; and, after a life-long struggle, a treaty of peace is concluded between the two rival powers. We may therefore be absolutely certain that the Cushite race at this period ruled over the ancient Hittite Empire from the Euphrates to Egypt, and consequently were designated as Khita or Hittites.

"The then Lord of Khita (Western Asia) Khita-sir, was the first to make to his Egyptian friends the proposal, written on a tablet of silver, for an offensive and defensive alliance. Ramses II. was prudent enough not to refuse such a proposal, and a treaty was made which laid the foundation of the intimate friendship so often mentioned by the Chroniclers of the time, between the two great empires of Asia and Africa." All the details of this treaty are handed down to us. We are indebted to Dr. Brugsch for a complete translation, and he tells us "In such a form, were peace and friendship made at

Brugsch, vol. ii. 70.

Philistines and Israelites.

Ramses, the City of Lower Egypt, between the two most powerful nations of the world."

Here then we have a treaty before us between the power of Egypt and the power of the Khita, the two most powerful nations in the world. It will be noticed that the territorial designations of these people give us no indication of their race, and Dr. Brugsch has failed to detect who they were. But can there be a doubt? Have we not prominently before us the two great Hamitic and Semitic races? Will the reader reflect for one moment and consider what other possible powers could be represented. Need I point out, that not only this great treaty, but the two greatest nations in the world are absolutely concealed in the Biblical narratives?

The solemn treaty concluded between Ramses II. and Khita-sir was cemented by a royal marriage; the Elamite Pharaoh, Ramses II., married a daughter of the Cushite King; this is very important to remember, for it united the two royal families in blood relationship, and it points out in a most convincing manner that only two races did exist in the empire, which is practically my sole contention. This is so important I will endeavour to strengthen my position.

It must be understood I do not wish to assert that there were two distinct and separate races, one ruling over Egypt, and one ruling in Western Asia; this was not at all the case; for the two races, to all appearance, were blended together over the entire empire, and could hardly be separated by a casual observer; nevertheless when revolutions took place and power changed hands, the two races, or perhaps we might rather call them parties, became sharply accentuated; this is no unusual development, it exists in our own country, and must always exist in every country where a foreign race has invaded and occupied it.

Conquest has no great influence on the mass of the people, they change their landlords, and pay their taxes to different collectors, that is about all; their social position is unchanged, but still in times

Philistines and Israelites.

of commotion the two parties separate under two distinct flags; so we must understand that in Egypt, and all the other territorial divisions in the empire, the two races permeated society, and could hardly be distinguished; just as the Normans and the Saxons can hardly be distinguished in England.

Henceforth we must notice that the Cushite and the Elamite kings will have a common ancestry; it does not however appear to have united the two races; but the reader will detect that it gives the Biblical writers a specious justification for claiming the reigning kings either as Jews or Israelities, that is Cushites or Elamites; and I shall point out that they have not neglected the advantage.

As it is not within the scope of my essay to develop history, I will not dwell upon details. Undoubtedly revolutions and stirring events took place soon after the iron hand of Ramses II. was removed; and it has been supposed that the exodus of slaves from Egypt took place about this period; not that we have any single record

Philistines and Israelites.

referring to such an event, but simply because there are recorded many serious disturbances about the period when Meneptah II. was reigning. It has, however, been convincingly proved that this Pharaoh was not drowned in the Red Sea, for his tomb has been discovered, and inscriptions have been found, which record that the Pharaoh was "blessed by *Amen* with a good old age, after a life-time of pleasure and a most prosperous reign." And the record ends by stating: "Thou hast gone before the Gods, the Victor, the Justified."

Brugsch, vol. ii. 143.

The following record reveals the political situation of the country: "Thus says King Ramses III. Hearken! I make you to know my glorious deeds, which I have performed as king of men. The people of Egypt lived in banishment abroad, so passed away long years; the land of Egypt belonged to princes of foreign parts. Other times came on afterwards, during years of scarcity. Arisu, a Phœnician, had raised himself among them to be a prince, and he compelled all the people to pay him

Philistines and Israelites.

tribute." We have here the Khita, that is the Cushites, dominating Egypt.

I will now refer to another inscription of considerable interest, for it informs us that Ramses III. inflicted a severe defeat on the Khita (Cushites), and we find him as far north as Cilicia and Carchemish, which guarded the northern fords of the Euphrates; so that at this period the Elamite Pharaoh must have held sway over the whole western empire.

According to a statement in the Harris papyrus, "Ramses III. erected in the land of Zahi (Philistia) a Ramesseum to Amen, in the city of Kanaan, a statue of the god was set up in its holy of holies in the name of the King." Here, then, we have an authentic record which proves beyond a doubt that the worship of Amen was followed in Palestine.

It is very remarkable that, although we are aware the influence of Egypt was so decided, not once in the Biblical records is there any allusion to their central symbols of worship. The names of their great Triad never appear; and yet, we may be

Brugsch, vol. ii. 164.

certain, that the Osirian cult exercised a widespread influence; and we learn from an inscription, only lately discovered, that the worship of Osiris, Horus, Isis and Bast flourished in Palestine down to the third century B.C.

<small>*Palestine Exploration, Quarterly Statement, April, 1892, p. 173.*</small>

Again, although we know that some great race occupied Palestine during the XVIIIth, XIXth, and XXth Egyptian dynasties, and that Set or Sutekh was their chief deity, not once is there any allusion to their names. This is very significant, and must force us to conclude that it did not suit the design of the priestly historian to refer to them.

<small>*Brugsch's Egypt, vol. i. 269.*</small>

Another inscription of the Elamite Pharaoh Ramses XII. leads us to infer that he ruled over the entire empire:—

<small>*Brugsch, vol. ii. 191.*</small>

"When the Pharaoh was in the river land of Naharain, *as his custom was every year*, the Kings of all the nations came with humility and friendship to the person of the Pharaoh. From the extremest ends of their countries they brought the gifts of gold, silver, blue and green stones; and all sorts of sweet smelling woods of the

Philistines and Israelites.

Holy Land were upon their shoulders; and each one endeavoured to outdo his neighbour."

A very remarkable record follows, which deserves careful attention.

"Then the King of Bakhatana brought his tribute, and placed at the head of it his eldest daughter, to honor [the] Pharaoh and to beg for his friendship. And the woman was much more beautiful to please Pharaoh than all other things. Then was the King's name written upon her, as the King's wife, Noferu-Ra. When the Pharaoh had come to Egypt everything was done for her which a queen required to use." *Brugsch, vol. ii. 191.*

Then follows a long record which tells us that the king of Bakhatana sent an envoy to the Pharaoh begging him to send a learned doctor to cure his daughter, who was possessed with an evil spirit. The doctor goes to Bakhatana but fails to cure her; so the King implores the Pharaoh to send Khonsu the oracular God of Thebes. Khonsu is carried to Bakhatana, a journey of seventeen months, with great pomp, and the King's daughter "becomes well on the spot."

Philistines and Israelites.

Does not this record let us behind the scenes? Dr. Brugsch, as well as E. de Rougé, very naturally identify Bakhatana with Ecbatana; but Dr. Brugsch adds, "this must be given up in the face of the fact that, in those times of the decay of the rule of the Ramesides, such distant towns and countries could not have been subject to the empire of the Pharaohs." But if the reader has followed me, it must be understood that the Ramessides represented the power of Elam; so we are absolutely forced to the conclusion, that Ramses XII. was an Elamite Pharaoh and ruled over an Empire extending from Ecbatana to Thebes. I must submit that this no longer can admit of a doubt. We must therefore understand that the solemn treaty dividing the Egyptian and Asiatic empires, concluded between the Elamite Pharaoh Ramses II. and the Cushite King Khita-sir, has been broken, and the Cushites have recognised the Elamite rule over the entire Empire.

The Elamites were now undoubtedly the greatest nation in the world.

Brugsch, vol. ii. 200.

We are approaching a great revolution,

Philistines and Israelites.

and the Egyptian inscriptions disclose that an *hereditary prince of Cush*, the High Priest of Amen, who bore the names of Smendes, Nisbindidi, and Hirhor, deposes the Ramessides, and founded the XXIst Egyptian dynasty. It becomes clear, then, that the Elamites have been overthrown, and the Cushites have succeeded to power ; consequently the Cushites are now the greatest nation in the world.

I must beg the reader to bear in mind that this is authentic history gathered from inscriptions, and accepted by all scholars ; and as Hirhor is disclosed as a Prince of Cush, he must have flown the Cushite flag.

We must remember that the Elamite Pharaoh, Ramses XII., ruled from Ecbatana to Thebes ; but as Hirhor only styles himself the Pharaoh of Egypt and Lord of the Ruthen (Western Asia), we must understand that the Elamite forces had been driven beyond the Euphrates, and Hirhor's Cushite flag was only paramount from the Euphrates to Ethiopia. The Elamites would still have been dominant on the east of the Euphrates.

CHAPTER III.

WE will now turn to the Biblical records of this period; but let us first clearly grasp the political situation. The Elamite Ramessides had been in power over the entire empire from Ecbatana to Thebes for more than a century, consequently the Elamite flag floated over every fortress in the empire; the word of Ramses XII. was law in Palestine.

I. Samuel xvii.

It is recorded that the Philistines under Achish, King of Gath, were in conflict with the Israelites. What, then, can this possibly disclose but a war in the empire? and, as I have shown that the Philistines were the Cushite Hyksos, it is manifest that Achish had thrown off his allegiance to the Elamite Pharaoh. The Philistines, therefore, must have been fighting under the Cushite flag, and the Israelites were withstanding them under the banner of Elam. And, when we

Philistines and Israelites. 49

find that King Achish defeated and disarmed the Israelites, it becomes glaringly manifest that Achish had hoisted the Cushite flag in Palestine and was defying the Elamite great King. *I. Samuel xiii. 19.*

We might then anticipate that the Pharaoh would move his forces into Palestine in order to crush the rebellion. Not one word, however, is found in the Biblical narratives which could lead us to infer that the Pharaoh was interested in the conflict; but two strange characters are introduced on the scene, who lead the Israelite forces against the Philistines; and we have it recorded that Saul, the son of Kish, who appears to have been his father's stable boy, was selected by the Israelites as their king, and David, the son of Jesse, a simple shepherd lad, becomes his general. *I. Samuel ix.*

I. Samuel xvii. 15.

I will not touch on details, but we gather that the war against the Philistines was carried on energetically. Saul slew his thousands and David his ten thousands. The Philistines are defeated; a peace is concluded, and they retire to their strong- *xix. 16.*

Philistines and Israelites.

I. Samuel xiv. 47.

holds on the sea coast. "So Saul took the Kingdom over Israel." Are we to suppose that two foreign races have been fighting for the crown, and the great King of Egypt is sitting idle on his throne?

xxvii. 2.

We now learn that war breaks out again; and it is recorded that David deserted Saul and went over to the Philistine camp. A general engagement soon takes place at Gilboa, where the Israelites are utterly

I. Samuel xxxi. 7.

defeated: "And when the men of Israel that were on the other side of the valley, and they that were on the other side of Jordan, saw that the men of Israel fled, and that Saul and his sons were dead, they forsook the cities and fled; and the Philistines came and dwelt in them." It becomes clear, then, that the Philistines have defeated the Israelites and are absolute masters of the country.

As we hear nothing more of King Achish, we must presume he fell in the battle; and we have it recorded that David was crowned King in Hebron.

II. Samuel ix. 9.

The battle of Gilboa was not decisive, for we find that Esh-baal, one of Saul's sons, is

Philistines and Israelites.

declared King over the Israelites. Under these circumstances we can only understand that David and Esh-baal have divided the Pharaoh's kingdom, and still not a word concerning the Pharaoh. *II. Samuel xi. 9.*

David, who had succeeded Achish as King of the Philistines, carries on the war. After seven and a half years of conflict he defeats the Israelites, murders their king Esh-baal, and the Israelites acknowledge his supremacy, which secures him a dominion, according to the Biblical records, from the Euphrates to Egypt. This is the divinely promised land. *iv. 6.* *viii. 3.*

As the inscriptions informs us that Ramses XII. exercised sovereignty from Ecbatana to Thebes, it appears very remarkable that a mere shepherd lad could have overthrown the power of the greatest nation in the world; and this becomes still more extraordinary when we find that the priestly writers entirely ignore the Ramesside power.

At first sight the priestly records appear utterly irreconcilable with the inscriptions, but this is not the case; we may assure ourselves that the compilers had authentic archives before them, and it enables us to detect the gross imposition they have foisted upon us; so let us take a bird's-eye view of the world's stage as disclosed by the inscriptions, which will glaringly expose the priestly plot.

It will be admitted that the great king Ramses XII. held dominion over Asia and Egypt; and, let it be remembered, that it was no transitory rule; his ancestors had reigned before him from generation to generation; his word was law over the whole empire.

Brugsch, vol. ii. 200.

The name of his grand vizier was Hirhor. He was the high priest of Amen, chief general of the army, and hereditary prince, king's son of Cush, the rival family of the reigning house of the Ramessides. The political situation is therefore apparent.

The inscriptions informs us that this Hirhor, king's son of Cush, usurped the throne of Egypt, and styled himself the King of Upper and Lower Egypt and Lord of the Ruthen, that is Western Asia.

Ibid. 202.

M. Maspero has lately discovered a Stele

Philistines and Israelites. 53

of this king Hirhor; he styles himself: "The good God, master of the two worlds, master of all action, Son of the Sun, master of diadems, Nsbindidi Miamun." Professor Sayce enables us to explain the significance of this title. <small>*Records of the Past (N. S.), vol. v. 19.*</small>

I have already pointed out that a Pharaoh of the name of Khuenaten had succeeded Amenhotep III., one of the Elamite Pharaohs of the XVIIIth Egyptian dynasty. This Pharaoh is not claimed by Seti as his ancestor, and as the records indicate a general revolution in art and religion, I ventured to assert that in Khuenaten we could detect the rise of the Cushite power. Khuenaten was a devoted worshipper of the Sun God, which strongly confirms my assertion.

Professor Sayce tells us his vizier, who stood next to the monarch and like him is addressed as "lord," bore the name of Dudu, the Dodo and David of the Old Testament. Hence Khuenaten's vizier was named David. <small>*Records of the Past (N. S.), vol. ii. 60.*</small>

And now we find that the vizier of Ramses XII, is named Nisbin-Didi; may I

Philistines and Israelites.

not add, the Didi, Dodo, and David of the Old Testament. Thus the vizier of Ramses XII. was also named David. This enables us to connect the priestly records with the inscriptions; the Biblical characters have merely been masked. Saul represents Ramses XII., and David personates his grand vizier. In the Biblical records, David, the shepherd lad, was the general of Saul's forces; he deserted to the Philistines, overthrew the house of Saul, and secured his kingdom. In the inscriptions, Hirhor (*i.e.* David), the king's son of Cush, was the general of the Elamite forces, he deserted to the Philistines, overthrew the Ramessides, and secured their empire. The records are practically identical.

The reader must notice that there can be no doubt as to the identity of the period under discussion. The fall of the Ramesside dominion over the empire, beyond a question, sychronises with the rise of David to power; and, as the inscriptions inform us, that the Pharaoh Hirhor, who deposed the Ramessides, bore the name of David, it becomes obvious that the Pharaoh Hirhor

II. Samuel viii. 3.

Philistines and Israelites.

was identical with the David of the Old Testament.

Beyond a doubt we have been hoodwinked and bamboozled by priestcraft. Instead of Abraham, Moses, and David being simple shepherds and vice-gerents of the Almighty, they were great Cushite Emperors and worshippers of the Sun God Masu, Aten, or Amen. I submit then that a flagrant imposition has been imposed upon us by the priestly writers, and let me add, by all sacerdotal historians; we are face to face with a widespread confederacy of imposture by no means confined to the Biblical narratives.

Before closing the chapter let me direct the reader's attention to David's lamentation over Saul; it is conceived in beautiful language, and is thus worthy of notice.

II. Samuel i. 17.

Now that we are aware that Ramses XII. has been paraded before us in the mask of Saul, and that David deposed him, and murdered all the members of his family, we can hardly credit that he lamented over his victim.

We learn from the inscriptions that

David (*i.e.* Hirhor), when vizier to Ramses XII., styled himself hereditary king's son of Cush; it stands to reason, then, that his father was alive; may we not recognise him in Achish the Cushite Philistine King of Gath? King Achish undoubtedly led the rebellion against the Pharaoh as the head of the house of Cush, and we can only conclude that he fell at Gilboa, leading his party to victory and empire. David, then, the hereditary king's son of Cush would naturally succeed him; so, if we can unmask Saul in David's lamentation, we shall disclose David weeping over his father Achish, the fallen warrior King of Cush.

If the reader will turn to this Biblical record, all the subtle distortions may be easily detected. The priestly combinations are certainly framed with consummate skill, but we may assure ourselves that our present conception of history is a monstrous delusion.

CHAPTER IV.

I HAVE pointed out that the power of the Elamite Pharaoh, Ramses XII., extended from Ecbatana to Thebes. The Elamite flag must, therefore, have floated over all the fortresses within the Eastern Empire. How is it possible, then, that David, according to the Biblical records, could have secured dominion from the Euphrates to Egypt without deposing the Pharaoh? When, therefore, the inscriptions disclose that Ramses XII. was deposed by his vizier, bearing the name of David, it becomes absolutely certain that the David of the Old Testament is identical with David, the vizier of Ramses XII. As David styles himself a prince of Cush, and the inscriptions inform us he ruled from the Euphrates to Ethiopia, it stands to reason that the flag of Cush now waved over all the fortresses, from the Euphrates to Ethiopia.

II. Samuel viii. 3.

Brugsch, vol. ii. 200.

Philistines and Israelites.

It will not be disputed that David was a lineal descendant of Abraham and Moses (*i.e.* Apepi) ; and as it is recorded that Abraham overthrew Chedorlaomer, the king of Elam, the two rival flags are very vividly before us ; and, as it will assist the reader in following my argument, I will trace them forward to the Roman occupation of the empire.

Genesis xiv.

List of dynasties ruling in Egypt from the XIIth dynasty to the Roman occupation of the empire, framed on the list of Pharaohs drawn up by Dr. Brugsch, to which I must refer the reader :—

Brugsch, vol. ii. 311.

Pharaoh of
Egypt— . Amenemhat I.   ⎫
Great King   to   ⎬ Semitic. XIIth Dynasty
of Elam . Chedorlaomer.   ⎭ Flag of Elam.

         Abraham   . ⎫
             to   ⎬ Hamitic. XIIIth „
Moses   . Apepi .   .   ⎭ Flag of Cush.

Hamitic exodus under Apepi (*i.e.* Moses).

Joseph . Aahmes .   . ⎫
          to   ⎬ Semitic. XIVth „
Amenhotep III.   ⎭ Flag of Elam.

Semitic exodus under Amenhotep.

Philistines and Israelites.

The Pharaoh "which knew not Joseph."	Khuenaten to Ai . . .	Hamitic. Flag of Cush.	XVth Dynasty.
	Horemhib to Mineptah	Semitic. Flag of Elam.	XVIth „
(Doubtful).	Seti II. . to Setnakht	Hamitic. Flag of Cush.	XVIIth „
Eshbaal	Ramses III. . to Ramses XIII.	Semitic. Flag of Elam.	XVIIIth „
David (Doubtful).	Hirhor . to Pisebkhan	Hamitic. Flag of Cush.	XIXth „
Isaiah	Shishak . to Usarkon	Semitic. Flag of Elam.	XXth „
Apries	Bokenranef to Uahabra	Hamitic. Flag of Cush.	XXIst „
Jeremiah .	Aahmes .	Semitic. Flag of Elam.	XXIInd „
Ishmael .	Psamethik III.	Hamitic. Flag of Cush.	XXIIIrd „

Cambyses to Darius II.	Semitic. Flag of Elam.	XXIVth Dyn.
Amyrtæus to Nakhtnebef	Hamitic. Flag of Cush.	XXVth ,,
Ochus to Darius.	Semitic. Flag of Elam.	XXVIth ,,
Alexander to Œgus	Hamitic. Flag of Cush.	XXVIIth ,,
Ptolemy Soter to Cleopatra	Semitic. Flag of Elam.	XXVIIIth ,,
Augustus Roman occupation	Hamitic. Flag of Cush.	XXIXth ,,

The reader will notice that this dynastic list discloses an entirely new historical view. It certainly receives no support from historians, and is apparently inconsistent with the Biblical narratives. But we must bear in mind that all our conceptions of ancient history have been derived from the priestly writers; hence, if it can be shown

Philistines and Israelites.

that the records themselves are inconsistent, the whole priestly fabric falls to the ground.

Perhaps the most important and unambiguous record handed down to us is that which informs us that the world was dominated by the three paramount races of Shem, Ham, and Japheth. Undoubtedly, then, the world's history must be centred in these three races. Is it not glaringly apparent that they have been obscured by the priestly writers?

My dynastic list, massively confirmed by authentic inscriptions, certainly discloses the dominant Semitic and Hamitic powers; and we might possibly discover the Japhetic race in the northern races, obscured under the names of Teutons, Slavs, Goths, and many other designations.

Let us now return to the great revolution which overthrew the Elamite power.

We certainly gather from the inscriptions that Ramses XII. ruled over the entire Eastern Empire; but it is more than probable that the high seat of government was in Elam or Ecbatana, and the Pharaoh was

Brugsch, vol. ii. 191.

a vassal to the Great King. We may therefore conclude, when David (*i.e.*, Hirhor) deposed the Ramessides and hoisted the Cushite flag from Carchemish to Ethiopia, that the Elamite power was still dominant on the east of the Euphrates. This is all-important to note, for the priestly historians would have us infer that a foreign race appears upon the scene. The Elamites on the east of the Euphrates are adroitly presented to us as Assyrians, leading us insensibly to infer that they were not Elamites. The reader will notice that the territorial designation very neatly obscures their race, which is vital to the priestly design. We must not however be led astray; beyond a shadow of doubt the Assyrians represented the Elamite flag. They had probably shifted their seat of Government to Nineveh, and became termed Assyrians. This is absolutely confirmed; for Asshur, who undoubtedly represents the Assyrian family, is recorded to have been the son of Elam.

Dr. Brugsch has fallen into the trap; for he connects the rise of the Assyrian power

Genesis x.—22.

Brugsch, vol. ii. 202.

Philistines and Israelites.

to a royal marriage with a Ramesside princess; this marriage undoubtedly did take place, but it was only an ordinary marriage between the Elamite royal families.

It will be remembered when David died that a struggle for the throne is recorded; hence it becomes clear that David held his own up to the time of his death. David's last psalm plainly indicates this; it was his death dirge, and is entitled a Psalm for Solomon:— *1. Kings xi.*

"Give the King thy judgments O God and thy righteousness unto the King's son. He shall judge thy people with righteousness and the poor with judgment. He shall have dominion also from sea to sea and from the river to the ends of the earth. They that dwell in the wilderness shall bow before him, and his enemies shall lick the dust. The Kings of Tarshish and of the isles shall bring presents; the Kings of Sheba and Seba shall offer gifts. Yea, all Kings shall fall down before him; all nations shall serve him; his name shall endure for ever; his name shall be continued as long as the sun, and men shall be *Psalms lxxii.*

Philistines and Israelites.

blessed in him; all nations shall call him blessed. Amen and Amen."

Such an eulogy could hardly apply to a petty King of Judea, reigning over a community of Hebrews which no historian or commentator has been able to define. We must not forget that David was High Priest of Amen, so it was only natural that he should conclude his prayer in the name of that Deity.

When, however, we have discovered that Saul represents the Elamite Pharaoh Ramses XII., and David personates the Cushite Pharaoh Hirhor who deposed him, we must depend on the monuments and inscriptions for historical guidance rather than the priestly narratives. Hence, as we gather from the inscriptions that Piankhi succeeded Hirhor (*i. e.*, David) on the throne of Egypt, we must conclude that David's dirge referred to Piankhi; and the name of Solomon is another subterfuge.

Brugsch, vol. ii. 203.

We learn from the inscriptions, when David (*i.e.*, Hirhor) overthrew the Ramessides, he banished the malcontents to an oasis; and we further gather, that in the

Philistines and Israelites.

twenty-fifth year of Piankhi's reign the banished Ramessides were recalled. Dr. Brugsch gives us a full translation of the important document which records it. He tells us: "that the recall of the exiles did not spring from any special goodness of heart, but was a politic measure to quiet the agitation fomenting in the country."

"While these events were taking place, which the inscriptions set forth, it appears that Naromath (Nimrod) the Great King of Assyria who had been associated on the throne by his father Shashanq, had advanced into Egypt with an army with the intention of conquering the country, and turning it into an Assyrian [Elamite] dependency. Here, in Egypt, death surprised him. His mother, Mehet-en-usekh, was in all probability a daughter of the XIVth Ramessu. According to her desire, her son, the great king of kings, was buried in Abydus, and the feasts of the dead were instituted in his honour. When Egypt had thus become virtually a province of the Assyrian [Elamite] Empire, Shashanq, the son of the great King Naromath, of whom we have just

Brugsch, vol. ii. 206.

spoken, was made King. These measures were evidently taken during the presence of the great king in Egypt. He visited Thebes, and did not fail to pay a visit to the grave of his beloved son at Abydus; he was bitterly chagrined at its neglected state; and the officials were all punished with death. These circumstances have been handed down to us in an inscription of unusual magnitude on the front side of a granite block at Abydus; and can be read without misunderstanding."

Brugsch, vol. ii. 211.

Dr. Brugsch gives us the translation, and adds: "This inscription is one of the most remarkable, and, I will add, one of the most surprising, ever found on Egyptian soil. Who could have expected such direct evidence of the presence of an Assyrian great king in the valley of the Nile, when the monuments had obstinately suppressed all information of the fact?"

Dr. Brugsch then goes on to inform us that these facts are confirmed by another inscription he discovered on a statue of the Great King Nimrod, which is exhibited in the middle of the chief hall of the Egyptian collection in Florence; and we are indebted to him for a full translation. *Brugsch, vol. ii. 213.*

Dr. Brugsch has not, however, explained their full significance. We are led to inquire who this great King of Assyria, so conspicuous on the monuments, could have been, and how it is we do not discover him in the royal lists. We may be certain that Naromath was the great Elamite King, and his identity has been designedly obscured.

The Cushites under David (*i.e.* Hirhor) had wrested Western Asia and Egypt from the Elamites some fifty or sixty years previously. This Naromath, then, must have recovered the empire from the house of David. A great revolution must have taken place. I submit with all confidence that this cannot be questioned, and it proves glaringly that the priestly narratives, although based upon a substratum of truth, convey an absolutely false conception of history. This becomes still more significant when we find that all modern priestly writers have supported them.

We must now understand that the Elamites have deposed the Cushites under the house of David (*i.e.* Hirhor), and have recovered their power over the entire empire from Ecbatana to Thebes; hence every petty king throughout the length and breadth of the land would fly the Elamite flag. We cannot, therefore, credit that the kings of Judea and Israel, both vassals of the Great King, could have been so frequently at war with each other as indicated in the Biblical narratives.

We must bear in mind that the Elamite and Cushite royal families were united in blood relationship; so we may expect to find the royal princes serving under both flags. The Cushite party, although out of power, were still formidable, and we find a junior branch of the house of David takes office under the Elamite flag.

Brugsch, vol. ii. 202.

Shishak, the son of the great Elamite King, was undoubtedly the head of the Elamite Ramesside house, and ascended the throne of Egypt by hereditary right.

1. Kings iii. 1.

Solomon, a younger son of David, allies himself with the Elamite Pharaoh Shishak, and becomes, so it is said, petty king of Judea, under the Elamite flag. This is confirmed,

Philistines and Israelites. 69

for we gather that the empire enjoyed peace during his long reign. It will be remembered that he was a younger son of David by Bath-Sheba. The story relating to David's marriage to Bath-Sheba is so absurd that we may dismiss it as fiction. Probably Bath-Sheba, as the name indicates, was a daughter of the king of Sheba; and, if we read between the lines of the priestly narratives, we might hazard a conjecture that Solomon succeeded to the throne of Sheba.

If we turn to the Koran we shall find Solomon is alluded to as a great monarch; he is presented to us as endowed with supernatural power. He had a carpet 500 parasangs long, on which was placed 300 thrones of gold and silver. He would bid the wind to raise the carpet, with all that was on it. In the morning he would be at Damascus, in the evening in Jerusalem, and the next day in the desert of Arabia. He went to Yemen, his route was by the Hedjaz; he arrives at Mecca, and predicts the coming of Mohammed; he visits and marries the queen of Saba; he converts her and all her army to the worship of Allah.

See Edwin Johnson, Rise of Christendom, 196.

Philistines and Israelites.

The transition from the Koran to the Biblical narrative is scarcely apparent, unless it is pointed out:—

I. Kings x. 13.

"And King Solomon gave unto the queen of Sheba all her desire, whatsoever she asked, beside that which Solomon gave her of his royal bounty. Now the weight of gold that came to Solomon in one year was six hundred three score and six talents of gold, beside that he had of the merchantmen, and of the traffic of the spice merchants, and of all the kings of Arabia, and of the governors of the country. Moreover the king made a great throne of ivory, and overlaid it with best gold. And twelve lions stood there on the one side and on the other upon the six steps; there was not the like made in any kingdom. And all King Solomon's drinking vessels were of gold, none were silver; it was nothing accounted of in the days of Solomon. For the king had at sea a navy of Tharshish with the navy of Hiram, bringing gold, and silver, ivory, and apes, and peacocks. So King Solomon exceeded all the kings of the earth for riches and

Philistines and Israelites. 71

for wisdom. And all the earth sought Solomon to hear his wisdom, which God had put into his heart. He had a thousand and four hundred chariots, and twelve thousand horsemen. And Solomon had horses brought out of Egypt, and a chariot came up and went out of Egypt for six hundred shekels of silver, and an horse for an hundred and fifty."

We may, therefore, gather from the Koran and the Bible, that Solomon was a powerful emperor. We can but inquire whether this was the petty king over the small province of Judea. We may further surmise that Solomon's relations with Arabia enabled him, with the aid of the Phœnicians, to secure great wealth through commercial enterprise. His son Rehoboam succeeds him on the throne of Judea. That he was a vassal of the great Elamite King is manifest, for he rebels against the Elamite power : "And it came to pass in the fifth year of King Rehoboam, that Shishak, King of Egypt, came up against Jerusalem ; and he took away the treasures of the house of the Lord, and the treasures of the King's

1. King. xiv. 25.

house; he even took away all. And he took away all the shields of gold which Solomon had made."

Here we have an historical event handed down to us, and many very thrilling incidents in connection with it are minutely recited; thus we are left to suppose that the writers had the fullest information to draw upon; and as we find this invasion of Judea by Shishak is recorded on the walls of Karnac at Thebes, we may be sure it was a successful and very important campaign. We may therefore safely conclude that it represents a wide spread rebellion, and shadows a hotly contested conflict for supremacy in the empire between the Cushite house of David (*i.e.*, Hirhor) and the Elamite house of Shishak.

The reader will notice that the Elamites are first obscured by referring to them as Assyrians; and, again, by alluding to the invasion of Judea by the Elamite Pharaoh, as the Pharaoh of Egypt; leading us insensibly to infer that he was a native Egyptian king, and that it was a war between Egypt and Judea.

Philistines and Israelites. 73

The combinations supporting the plot are truly admirable!

We gather from the Biblical records that Shishak did not depose Rehoboam, but merely put him under tribute and concluded a peace. So we may infer that Rehoboam still represents a powerful party, but now served under the Elamite flag: "Now the acts of Rehoboam, first and last, are they not written in the book of Shemaiah the prophet, and of Iddo the seer, concerning genealogies? And there were wars between Rehoboam and Jeroboam continually." *II. Chron. xii. 12.*

This record explains the sources from whence the compilers derived their information, and, as it could hardly be termed a Divine inspiration, we can only inquire what has become of these priceless archives.

The records also inform us that the struggle for supremacy in the Empire between the two great parties continued with unabating energy. As Rehoboam and Jeroboam were both vassals to the great Elamite King, a war between them must certainly disclose a conflict for supremacy between the Semitic and Hamitic races.

CHAPTER V.

It will be remembered when the Cushites under David (*i.e.* Hirhor) overthrew the Elamite Ramessides, the malcontents were banished to an oasis. It was only natural then, when the Elamite Assyrians came into power, that they should banish the Cushite malcontents; and we learn from the inscriptions that they retired to their dominion in Ethiopia, and are designated as kings of Cush. This was no new title, as Hirhor (*i.e.* David) styled himself a king's son of Cush before he supplanted the Elamites.

Solomon, a younger branch of the Cushite house of David, it is true, had made terms with his conquerors and had elected to serve as King of Judea under the Elamite flag. I have pointed out that his son Rehoboam had rebelled against the Elamite rule, and the Elamite Pharaoh, Shishak, had invaded Judea and put him under tribute as

Brugsch, vol. ii. 234.

I. Kings ii. 1.

II. Chron. xii. 12.

Philistines and Israelites.

his vassal. The Elamite flag must, therefore, have floated over Jerusalem, and his son Abijah must have sworn allegiance to the great king in Nineveh before he succeeded to the throne.

"And Abijah waxed mighty, and married fourteen wives, and begat twenty and two sons and sixteen daughters. So Abijah slept with his fathers, and they buried him in the city of David: and Asa his son reigned in his stead. In his days the land was quiet ten years." *II. Chron. xiii. 21.*

Asa succeeds to the throne in peace, "and he built fenced cities in Judah, for the land had rest and he had no war in those days." The Elamite flag must, therefore, have still floated over the fortresses from Nineveh to Thebes. This is amply confirmed, for it is recorded that the Elamite army numbered 540,000 mighty men of valour. The priestly writers ingeniously lead us to infer that these forces were under the independent command of Asa.

We now come to another revolution, and are again insidiously led to believe that a new power comes on the scene:—"And

II. Chron. xiv. 9.

there came out against them Zerah the Ethiopian with an host of a thousand thousand and three hundred chariots. Then Asa went out against him, so the Lord smote the Ethiopians before Asa and before Judah, and the Ethiopians fled."

The reader will notice it is recorded that the Ethiopians fled before Asa, and Judah; are not the two rival parties here distinctly defined? It must be remembered that Solomon was David's youngest son, hence Asa was only a junior branch of David's family.

When the Elamites under Shishak secured dominion, the Cushite royal family retired to their dominion in Ethiopia; but Solomon accepted office under Shishak, and his family had considered it prudent to continue his policy. We may, however, presume that Asa still led a considerable Cushite following, who supported his family from motives of personal interest; hence the writers dimly distinguish the Cushite and Elamite forces under Asa. It assists the priestly plot, and is admirably adapted to create confusion; for unless we thoroughly understand the political position, we must feel surprise that Zerah, the undoubted head of the Cushite party, should be attacking the Cushite Asa. The geographical position of this battle has not been ascertained, but Zerah must certainly have been the reigning Cushite king of the house of David (*i.e.* Hirhor) in Ethiopia. We could hardly credit that the Cushites, so lately fugitives, were powerful enough to re-conquer Egypt. As this battle is not recorded in the Book of Kings as one of the exploits of Asa, we may shrewdly surmise that it is interpolated in the Book of Chronicles to give importance to the petty king of Judea; we may therefore conjecture that this battle took place in Upper Egypt.

The reader will notice how artfully the records are put before us; for we are led insidiously to presume that the Ethiopians were a Negro race and a new power on the scene; whereas they represented, beyond a doubt, the Cushites who had been supplanted by the Elamites in Egypt and had retired to Ethiopia.

I must again point out that the term

Ethiopian is only a territorial designation, and gives no indication of race; we can only admire the neatness of the combination in the priestly plot, for it is practically true, and yet completely obscures true history. The revolution, then, discloses another struggle for empire by the Cushite house of David (*i.e.* Hirhor).

Solomon, Rehoboam, Abijah, and Asa, the petty kings of Judea of the house of Solomon, had clearly reigned under the Elamite flag; they were, beyond a doubt, all vassals to the great Elamite king in Nineveh, and were forced to oppose the rising of the house of Cush from Ethiopia.

It would, however, appear to have been a general rising, for Asa is disclosed in conflict with the Cushites in Judea, and he drove them into their strongholds on the sea coast. It becomes clear, then, that the Cushite rebellion was unsuccessful. The Elamite dynasty of Shishak still ruled in Egypt. The reader must, however, note that the Philistine Cushites still hold their strongholds on the sea coast.

Zerah probably concluded a peace, be-

II. Chron. xiv. 13

Philistines and Israelites.

came tributary to the Pharaoh, and retired to Ethiopia.

M. Naville throws a glimmer of light on this part of history. Describing the long procession recorded on the ruined walls of the temple of Bubastis (which I personally inspected under his able guidance), he tells us:—" Thus we see that Osorkon brought to his festival men from the Upper Nile. They are not the only specimens of African races. .... They look like the genuine Egyptians, although they were of a foreign race ; we have here a proof of the dislike which the Egyptians felt towards the negro tribe, unless they had to represent captives or vassals paying tribute. Here the Nubians are like priests ; they are fulfilling a sacred office, therefore their strange type must not be indicated. It is quite possible that in many cases we go astray, not knowing that the representation which we see is merely conventional, and does not give us the real type of the person which would betray his origin. A striking instance of the errors which we are apt to commit was given by the discovery made in Syria, at Sendjerli, of

Festival Hall of Osorkon, ii., Edouard Naville, page 22.

the great tablet relating the conquests of Esarhaddon, where we see the king Tahraka pictured as a negro. It is clear that in this case it is Esarhaddon's sculpture which is reliable and true. The Assyrian king would not have represented Tahraka as a negro if he had not been so. But the hieroglyphical inscriptions of Tahraka, and his sculptures, not only leave us in absolute ignorance of this fact, but would lead us to consider him as an Egyptian of pure blood. Why did Osorkon wish that Ethiopians should be present at his festival in the Delta? Had he any special connection with Ethiopia by birth or by conquest? These are questions to which we can give no answer."

The reader must notice that M. Naville's questions can now be answered. The indigenous Ethiopians were undoubtedly negroes, but the people who held dominion over them were the Cushites; and, we may surmise, that the strange man we see in the procession is a Cushite; and, as Osorkon II. may very well sychronise with Zerah, we may have Zerah himself before us. He is clearly not a negro!

Philistines and Israelites.

We may be almost certain that the Cushites were much darker than the Elamites; so we might account for Esarhaddon exaggerating Tahraka's complexion out of derision. We might also surmise that it was the dark work of the forger.

Esarhaddon, in his cylinder, refers to Tahraka as "King of Cush." This unquestionably discloses that Tahraka of the house of David (*i.e.* Hirhor) was a Cushite and flying the Cushite flag.

George Smith, Assyrian Eponym, 142.

We may gather from the narratives that Asa had adopted the Elamite flag both politically and religiously; but we must bear in mind he was half Elamite by birth owing to royal marriage alliances. It becomes evident that he suppressed the Cushite cult:—" And he gathered all Judah and Benjamin, and the strangers with them out of Ephraim and Manasseh, and out of Simeon; for they fell to him out of Israel in abundance, when they saw that the Lord his God was with him"—(*i.e.* the Elamite Great King).

II. Chron. xv. 9.

I must submit that this record plainly indicates that there were two distinct parties; and it is evident that Asa was considered a Cushite; for, had he been recognised as an Elamite, it would not have needed recording that the Israelites (Elamites) "fell to him out of Israel in abundance" when the Cushite cult had been suppressed. The very fact that a cult was suppressed proves that two rival religions existed. It further leads us to conclude that the Cushite party were now in a hopeless minority. They had just rebelled and had suffered a severe defeat.

But the truth plainly leaks out as we follow the records; for we learn that Maachah, King Asa's mother, still followed her family worship, and was accordingly deposed as Queen.

II. Chron. xv. 16.

"But the high places were not taken away out of Israel; nevertheless Asa was perfect all his days." He had gone over body and soul to the Elamites, "and the country rested in peace during twenty years," under the Elamite flag.

War again breaks out. "In the six and thirtieth year of the reign of Asa, Baasha King of Israel came up against Judah, and

II. Chron. xvi. 1.

Philistines and Israelites.

built Ramah to the intent that he might let none go out or come in to Asa King of Judah." Here then, the two races are prominently before us and again in conflict. "Then Asa brought out silver and gold out of the treasures of the house, and sent to Ben-hadad King of Syria that dwelt at Damascus, saying, there is a league between me and thee, as there was between my father and thy father   reak thy league with Baasha King of   , that he may depart from me."

The records I have   amply prove that the Great Elamite ...ng in Nineveh held dominion over the united empire extending from Elam to Thebes; it follows that the petty Kings of Judea and Israel and all the kings within the empire were vassals to the Great King. Under these circumstances we can only conclude, that the war between Asa King of Judea and Baasha King of Israel, only discloses another Cushite rebellion.

II. Chron. xvi.

CHAPTER VI.

As it is not my task to develop history, we may now pass over some two hundred years; but let us carefully bear in mind that Naromath or Nimrod, the great Elamite king, had soon after the death of David recovered possession of the empire. It stands to reason, then, that he must have deposed David's flag, forcing the Cushite troops to retire to their dominion in Ethiopia. The flag of Elam would have flown over every fortress within the empire from Nineveh to Thebes.

Shishak, the son of the Great King, is placed on the throne of Egypt; and we may be absolutely certain that Shishak, as well as every petty king throughout the length and breadth of the empire, were vassals of the Great King, and flew the Elamite flag; and I will further contend that the name attributed to this Pharaoh,

Brugsch, vol. ii. 211.

Ibid. 234.

Philistines and Israelites.

as disclosed by his cartouches, is neither Shishak nor Sheshanq, but Sargon, as closely as hieroglyphics could express it. His name has been subtly distorted in order to obscure the Elamite dominion.

We must then understand that all the petty kings of Judea and Israel, during the Elamite Assyrian rule, which lasted some two hundred and fifty years, were vassals to the Great Elamite King. Many rebellions are recorded in Western Asia, and the Great King has himself to head his forces in suppressing them.

The Cushites under the house of David (*i.e.* Hirhor), had recovered from their signal defeat under Zerah; and a Pharaoh of the name of Bochoris looms dimly on the horizon. He advanced from Ethiopia, and undoubtedly was a descendant of Zerah and a Cushite of the house of David (*i.e.* Hirhor.) As the inscriptions inform us he secured the throne of Egypt, we can only conclude that he deposed the Elamite Pharaoh.

The records of this period are so confused I will not dwell upon them, but pass to the reign of the Pharaoh Sabakah, the So of the priestly writers. It must, however, be distinctly remembered, that this Pharaoh was also a descendant of the Cushite house of David (*i. e.* Hirhor), and in no sense an Ethiopian negro as the writers would have us believe.

At this period then the flag of Cush must have been paramount in Egypt and Ethiopia. The flag of Elam still floated over every fortress in the Asiatic empire.

When Sabakah had deposed the Elamite Pharaoh Usargon and consolidated his kingdom, we may be sure he followed up his victory and carried his arms into Western Asia. This is solidly confirmed, for we find that Hoshea, the Elamite petty king of Israel, has become his tributary.

II. Kings xvii. 4

Hezekiah, of the House of Solomon, was petty king of Judea and vassal to the Great Elamite king; this is most important to notice, for it proves, beyond a doubt, that the Assyrian Elamites had continued their rule over the empire since the time of Shishak, a period of some two hundred and fifty years; but when we find it recorded

II. Kings xviii.

Philistines and Israelites.

that on the rise of the Cushite power, under Sabakah, Hezekiah "rebelled against the Great King and served him not," it becomes evident that the Cushites under Sabakah had become masters of Judea and Israel, which is now alluded to as Samaria; they must, therefore, have defeated the Elamites, and the flag of Cush would have replaced the Elamite flag over Jerusalem and Samaria.

But let us clearly understand, when the Elamite King Shalmaneser invades the country in order to recover his dominion, it undoubtedly represents a war between the Elamites and the Cushites. There cannot be a question of doubt that Sabakah of the house of David (*i.e.* Hirbor) had taken Samaria and Jerusalem, and that they were both garrisoned by Sabakah's troops.

I must again remind the reader that the two great rival races permeated every province of the empire. The term Israelite is merely a territorial designation for the people residing within the province of Israel; hence the term Israelite would apply equally to both Cushites and Elamites.

Philistines and Israelites.

The priestly writers, taking advantage of this, have confounded the two races together; it is one of the brilliant combinations in their plot, for it insensibly obscures the two races in conflict.

II. Kings xviii. 9.

It is recorded that Shalmaneser King of Assyria [the Elamite Great King] came up against Samaria and besieged it. There is no record that Shalmaneser succeeded in taking Samaria; on the other hand, we are told, that at the end of three years *they* took it; and we gather from the inscriptions that Shalmaneser did not take it, but that he was killed, or died, during the blockade; and Sargon, who succeeded him as the Great King, conducted the successful assault.

Professor Sayce, Fresh Light from the Monuments, 106.

Professor Sayce tells us that Sargon was one of the Assyrian generals; may we not surmise who this Sargon was? We are aware that when the Elamite Assyrians secured possession of the Empire by deposing the Cushite house of David, Shishak the Great King's son, was placed on the throne of Egypt, and his dynasty had succeeded him in unbroken succession. It follows that these Pharaohs were all of the royal Elamite Assyrian family. The Pharaoh deposed by Bochoris or Sabakah is known to us on the lists as Usargon; and, as this deposed Pharaoh would certainly be associated with Shalmaneser in the siege of Samaria, we may reasonably conjecture that Usargon succeeded Shalmaneser as the great Elamite King; and, as we find that Isaiah was by far the most commanding character in the Biblical scene, at this period, we might be led to surmise that Isaiah and Sargon were identical personages.

The priestly writers, and all their commentators, would have us believe that the Israelites were taken away into captivity, on the fall of Samaria, and that they were the chosen people of the Almighty. It is a most subtle combination and calculated to deceive the very elect. We may, however, be absolutely certain that the Israelites were not a distinct nation; they simply represented the people residing in the province of Israel, just as Yorkshiremen represent the people residing in Yorkshire, and when we recog-

Philistines and Israelites.

nise that the Cushites and Elamites permeated through the province, it becomes obvious that there were Cushite Israelites and Elamite Israelites within the province; precisely as Yorkshire Tories and Yorkshire Radicals are found in the county of York. Let us, however, carefully remember that the Elamite section of the Israelites are supposed to be God's chosen people, and the Cushite section are Philistines under the ban of the Almighty. When, therefore, the Elamite king Sargon recaptured Samaria from the Cushite Pharaoh Sabakah, his prisoners certainly were Cushites; and we are led to infer that he took into captivity or expelled all the Cushites in the province and brought in Elamites whom he could depend upon to take their place; thus, instead of the chosen people of priestcraft being taken into captivity on the fall of Samaria they came into power; and it was their enemies, the so-called Philistines, who suffered defeat. I must submit that this in itself exposes the priestly plot; will the reader pause for a moment's reflection?

The Great Elamite King follows up his

Philistines and Israelites.

victory, besieges Jerusalem, hauls down the Cushite flag, and places the country under tribute. The Elamites are now again masters of the Asiatic empire, and a peace is probably concluded. The Cushite Philistine forces retire to their strongholds on the sea-coast, and the main army, under the Pharaoh Sabakah, retreated to Egypt.

As soon as the Elamite forces of the Great King retired to Assyria the Cushites under Sabakah recover possession of Jerusalem, and again the Great Elamite King besieges the fortress. It stands to reason that Sabakah must have occupied it, or the Elamites would have had no cause to besiege it.

I must leave it to scholars to unravel the ambiguous records; but it is very apparent that the two rival races were in continual conflict; and, as I have conclusively proved, that there were only two rival races within the empire, we may assure ourselves that Berodach-baladan, who is disclosed in conflict with the great Elamite King on the east of the Euphrates, was warring under the flag of Cush. His embassy to

II. King xx. 12.

Hezekiah certainly confirms this; and when we learn that Hezekiah again threw off his allegiance to the Great King we can only conclude that the Cushite flag again waved over Jerusalem. This is also confirmed, for we find that Sargon again invades the country and captures the strong fortress of Ashdod, which was in the possession of the Philistines.

Isaiah xx.

A few years after this invasion Sargon dies, and is succeeded by Sennacherib. The records inform us that he also invaded Western Asia, and attacked Jerusalem, which must have been still held by Hezekiah, so Hezekiah must at this period have flown the Cushite flag as vassal to the Pharaoh Tirhakah.

II. Kings xix. 35.

The reader must remember that Tirhakah is referred to in the Assyrian inscription as the King of Cush.

The Assyrian Eponym Canon, 142.

Jerusalem is closely blockaded, and Hezekiah sends to Isaiah, who certainly was a great Elamite potentate, and Isaiah tells Hezekiah that Sennacherib will raise the siege; he had undoubtedly been informed that the Cushite forces under

Philistines and Israelites.

Tirhakah were approaching. "And it came to pass that night, that the angel of the Lord went out, and smote in the camp of the Assyrians an hundred four score and five thousand: and when they arose early in the morning, behold, they were all dead corpses." May we not venture a conjecture, that the Cushites under Tirhakah had engaged the Elamites and almost annihilated them?

"So Sennacherib, king of Assyria, departed, and went and returned and dwelt in Nineveh." This invasion of the great Elamite King Sennacherib is confirmed by the inscriptions.

We are indebted to Professor Sayce for a translation of Sennacherib's tablet:— "Zedekiah, king of Ashkelon (says Sennacherib), who had not submitted to my yoke —himself, his daughters, and his brothers, the seed of the house of his fathers—I removed, and I sent him to Assyria. In the course of my campaign I approached and captured Beth-Dagon, Joppa, Beneberak, and Azur, the cities of Zedekiah, which did not submit at once to my yoke,

Fresh Lights from the Monuments, 114.

and I carried away their spoil. The priests, the chief men, and the common people of Ekron, who had thrown into chains their king Padi because he was faithful to his oaths to Assyria, and had given him up to Hezekiah the Jew, who imprisoned him like an enemy in a dark dungeon, feared in their hearts. The King of Egypt, the bowmen, the chariots, and the horses of the King of Ethiopia had gathered together innumerable forces and gone to their assistance. In sight of the town of Eltekeh was their order of battle drawn up ; they called their troops (to the battle). Trusting to Assur, my Lord, I fought with them and overthrew them. My hands took the captains of the chariots and the sons of the King of Egypt, as well as the captains of the chariots of the King of Ethiopia. I approached and captured the towns of Eltekeh and Timnath, and I carried away their spoil. I marched against the city of Ekron, and put to death the chief men who had committed the sin (of rebellion), and I hung up their bodies on stakes all round the city. I had Padi, their king, brought out from the midst of

Jerusalem. But as for Hezekiah of Judah, who had not submitted to my yoke, forty-six of his strong cities, together with innumerable fortresses and small towns which depended on them, by overthrowing the walls and open attack, by battle-engines and battering rams I beseiged, I captured. I brought out from the midst of them and counted as spoil 200,150 persons, great and small, male and female, horses, mules, asses, camels, oxen, and sheep without number. Hezekiah himself I shut up like a bird in a cage in Jerusalem, his royal city. I cut off his cities which I had spoiled from the midst of his land, and gave them to Metinti, king of Ashdod, Padi, king of Ekron, and Zil-baal, king of Gaza, and I made his country small."

We gather from this tablet that the great Elamite king was engaged in war with Tirhakah, the Cushite Pharaoh of Egypt. There can be no doubt that Tirhakah flew the Cushite flag, for he is styled, in Assyrian inscriptions, as King of Cush.

The reader will notice that Sennacherib pointedly alludes to Hezekiah as the Jew.

It is clear, then, that the Jews were defending Jerusalem. These Jews must therefore represent a section of the Cushite power; and as it is apparent that the great Elamite king was attacking all the fortresses on the sea coast which were held by the Philistines, may we not be certain that the Philistines represent the Cushite Jews? The Elamite Jews of the tribe of Judah, who also occupied Judea, were undoubtedly supporting their great King. Hence we have the conflict clearly defined, between Sennacherib, the great Elamite king, and the Cushite Pharaoh Tirhakah. The same races are contending for supremacy which met under the Cushite Abraham and the Elamite Chedorlaomer; which met under the Cushite Moses and the Elamite Aahmes; which met under the Cushite David and the Elamite Ramses. Clearly there were only two flags in the Empire.

We certainly hear of a race called the Amorites in the Biblical records, and the inscriptions disclose such a race; but they have long since passed out of ken, and Biblical historians, although they dwell

Philistines and Israelites.

upon them very tenaciously, cannot define them.

I submit, then, that there were only two paramount races engaged in conflict within the vast Eastern Empire, and let us understand that they were each animated with a spirit of bitter hostility. This is deserving of careful attention, for the priestly writers would have us believe that the Jews and the Israelites were one and the same race, and distinct from any other. I refer to the Cushite Philistine Jews, and the Elamite Jews of the tribe of Judah, who represent the Hamitic and Semitic races.

We now gather from the records that Sennacherib was murdered, and a war of succession takes place; but we must bear in mind that there are only two parties in the Empire; hence the fight for the crown would certainly be between the Cushites and the Elamites. This is amply confirmed, for we find that the Cushite Pharaoh, Tirhakah, has been firmly seated on the throne of Egypt for over twenty years, and has withstood all the attacks made by the Elamite kings against Jerusalem. The

Cushite flag probably flew over every fortress from Carchemish to Ethiopia.

There can be no doubt that the Elamites were eventually victorious; Esarhaddon secures the throne under the Elamite flag, and very shortly after invades Western Asia, and plants his flag on the fortress of Jerusalem, under his vassal Manasseh. We must remember that the two royal families were united in blood relationship, which explains how Manasseh of the junior house of Solomon took service under the Elamite flag. It becomes clear that Tirhakah still ruled over the fortresses on the sea coast of Judea, for the records inform us that Esarhaddon, some seven years after, takes Askelon, and drives Tirhakah out of Egypt into Ethiopia; so now the Elamite flag must have flown over every fortress from Elam to Thebes. In the following year Tirhakah invades Egypt from Ethiopia, but is defeated, and twenty satraps are set up in Egypt under the Elamite flag.

The records inform us that Esarhaddon had appointed Manasseh as King of Judea; we may be certain, however, that Manasseh

Assyrian Eponym, 201.

rebelled, and ran up the Cushite flag over Jerusalem: "Wherefore the Lord brought upon them the captains of the host of the King of Assyria, which took Manasseh among the thorns, and bound him with fetters and carried him to Babylon." This certainly indicates that Esarhaddon had crushed a Cushite rebellion. We can only conclude that when Esarhaddon had expelled Tirhakah from Egypt, a peace was concluded; Manasseh is released and reinstated on the throne of Judea under the Elamite flag.

II. Chron. xxxiii. 11.

On the death of Esarhaddon war again breaks out, and Tirhakah reconquers Egypt.

Assurbanipal succeeds Esarhaddon as the Great Elamite King, invades Egypt and expels the Cushite forces to Ethiopia. In the following year the Cushites again invade Egypt, but are repulsed, and the Cushite general, Necho, is taken captive.

Tirhakah now dies; and, as the inscriptions tell us that Urdamaneh succeeds to the throne of Egypt, it becomes clear that the Cushites were still in power in Egypt. This is confirmed; for we gather from the inscriptions that they carried their arms into Western Asia, and even attacked the Great King in his royal city of Nineveh; hence, at this period, the Cushite flag must have floated over all the fortresses from Carchemish to Ethiopia. This is absolutely confirmed by the inscriptions. We are indebted to Dr. Brugsch for the information. He gives us a translation of Assurbanipal's tablet: "In my first expedition I went against Egypt and Meroe. Tarquu, the King of Egypt and Ethiopia, whom Assarhaddon, the father who begat me, had subdued, returned out of his land. The kings, satraps, and generals, whom Assarhaddon, my father, had set over the Kingdom of Egypt, were driven out by him. They betook themselves to Nineveh. Against such deed my heart was moved and my bile was stirred up." I must refer the reader to Dr. Brugsch's long translation, but it informs us that Assarhaddon, although generally successful, was engaged in constant hostilities with the Kings of Cush.

I must submit that this conclusively proves my assertion that only two great

Brugsch, vol. ii. 267.

dominant races existed within the empire. As I have illustrated this in Chapter IV., by giving the Egyptian dynasties, I need not further enlarge upon it; but the reader will notice that if only two races are contending for supremacy in the empire, it stands to reason that the two provinces of Judea and Israel were simply ciphers in the politicial organization of the vast empire; hence, the priestly narratives give us a false impression of eastern history.

We may be absolutely certain that the worship practised in Judea and Israel was identical with that of their Great King; the reader will notice that this is adroitly concealed in the priestly narratives.

NOTE.—We have been hoodwinked by priestcraft: Judea and Israel were not isolated kingdoms, but small provinces in a vast empire, just as they are at the present moment, and just as they have been since the time of Abraham. It is inconsistent with reason to suppose an independent king could hold Judea, the gate of Asia and Africa. Such a position would enable him to tax all merchandise passing through his territory; and taxation is the symbol of supremacy, and can only be enforced by a Sovereign Power. A King of Judea could not have assumed such a position against the powers of Egypt, Carchemish, and Assyria.

CHAPTER VII.

WE learn from the inscriptions that Assur-bani-pal succeeded Esar-haddon as the Great Elamite King, and as we find him engaged in conflict with Urdamaneh, the Cushite Pharaoh of Egypt, we may assure ourselves that the struggle for supremacy between the two rival races is as hotly contested as ever. Dr. Brugsch tells us that "A thick veil covers the ensuing times in which the Ethiopians occupy the foreground of Egyptian history." But when we recognise that these so-called Ethiopians were the Cushites under the ancient house of Abraham, the veil is lifted and true history becomes revealed.

The inscriptions inform us that Assur-bani-pal's campaign against the Cushite Pharaoh Urdamaneh was a successful one, and as we find that Assur-bani-pal styles himself "King of Upper and Lower Egypt and Nubia," we can only conclude that

Brugsch, vol. ii. 275.

Ibid. 276.

Philistines and Israelites.

the flag of Elam now waved over every fortress from Elam to Napata. The Semitic race is now clearly dominant over the whole eastern empire; but their success is only short lived, for Psamethik I. succeeds, by the aid of his kindred, the Lacedemonians, in securing supremacy in Egypt, and assumes the double crown, which might perhaps represent the crowns of the two rival races. Dr. Brugsch informs us that Psamethik's name belonged to the Ethiopic family, to which he most probably owed his success; so we may certainly follow him as a descendant of the Cushite house of David (*i.e.* Hirhor). His title, Son of the Sun, recalls his ancestors, Moses, Khuenaten, and David, who all bore a similar designation.

1. Maccabees xii. 21.

Brugsch, vol. ii. 285.

Let me again remind the reader when the Elamite Assyrians overthrew the dynasty of David (*i.e.* Hirhor), and the elder branch of the royal family with their forces retired to Ethiopia, Solomon, David's youngest son, elected to take service under the Elamite flag.

It will be noticed that the priestly writers

have ingeniously obscured the elder branch of David's family by alluding to them as Ethiopians when they again come into power.

The inscriptions inform us that Hirhor (*i.e.* David), was a prince of Cush, and as Psamethik was one of his lineal descendants, he must have secured his accession to the throne of Egypt under the Cushite flag.

Whatever claims Psamethik might have had to the throne, he settled the dispute by marrying Shep-en-apet, the daughter and heiress of the Cushite Pharaoh Piankhi and his beautiful queen Ameniritis, which restored peace and order in the distracted relations of the royal succession. We must therefore understand that the Cushites had expelled the Elamite forces from Egypt, and Psamethik now ruled in undisputed sovereignty as the Cushite Pharaoh of the house of David (*i.e.* Hirhor). I must leave it to students to reconcile conflicting dates, and will pass over Psamethik's undoubtedly glorious reign.

Brugsch, vol. ii. 281.

Philistines and Israelites.

He is succeeded by Necho; and, as it would appear that Josiah was at this period petty king of Judea and vassal to the great Elamite king, it becomes evident that neither Psamethik's nor Necho's rule, at this period, extended beyond Egypt.

The Pharaoh Necho carries his arms into Asia; and, as we might anticipate, he comes into conflict with Josiah; a battle is recorded at Megiddo, where Josiah is slain, and the Elamite forces are completely routed. The Pharaoh pushes on his victory; and, as we find him at Carchemish, which guarded the northern fords of the Euphrates, we may be certain that he had expelled the Elamite forces from Western Asia. *II. Kings xxiii. 29.*

A great battle takes place at Carchemish between the Pharaoh Necho and the great Assyrian Elamite king. As this battle is recorded on the Egyptian monument we may assure ourselves that the victory rested with Necho; and, we may further surmise, that he not only took Carchemish, but Nineveh also, and planted his flag on the walls of Babylon.

The reader will probably consider this

a very daring assertion; but I still assert it with every confidence; for, as there were only two parties struggling for supremacy in the empire, it follows that if Nabopolassar, the great Elamite king, had to reconquer his kingdom, it must have previously been wrested from him by the Cushites. History, then, explains itself.

We learn from the records, that when the Cushite Pharaoh Necho returned from his victorious campaign, he appointed Jehoiakim as his vassal king of Judea. It is recorded that he reigned eleven years in Jerusalem, which proves that the country was at peace during this period; and, as we learn that Nebuchadnezzar, the son of the great Elamite king, recovered Nineveh from the Cushites, and then took the fortress of Carchemish, it stands to reason that the successful campaign of the Pharaoh Necho was previous to these events; hence, we must conclude, that the fall of the Cushite power and the rise of Elam occurred during the reign of the Pharaoh Apries.

I am perfectly aware that this view discloses an entirely new historical phase, and

II. Chron. xxxvi. 5.

receives no support from historians; but let us remember that all our knowledge of history has been derived through the priestly class. As Cardinal Newman observed, "we have been simply at their mercy." May we not, however, shrewdly conjecture that the Cardinal only ventured this apparently genuine confession with a view of giving the Church a loophole of escape, when awkward facts became only too conspicuous.

The Biblical narratives are, beyond a doubt, based upon authentic facts; these facts have only been adroitly distorted for the purpose of conveying an entirely different meaning. We have, therefore, only to eliminate the distortions, and the truth is revealed. This becomes comparatively easy when we discover the design, and the truth becomes established when we find it confirmed by long concealed documents beyond priestly control.

I have pointed out that the Cushite flag, under the Pharaoh Necho, must have been paramount from Babylon to Ethiopia; and, as we learn from the inscriptions, that Nabopolassar recovered his dominion on the east of the Euphrates, we may presume that this revolution occurred on the death of Necho.

Nabopolassar follows up his conquest and recaptures Carchemish, which must have been garrisoned by Cushite troops under the Pharaoh Apries. This opened the high road into Western Asia.

Nabopolassar dies, and is succeeded by his son Nebuchadnezzar as the great Elamite king; and very shortly after we find Nebuchadnezzar sacks the fortress of Jerusalem, deposes Jehoiakim, the Cushite petty king of Judea, and places Jehoiakin his son on the throne, under the Elamite flag.

The reader will notice that we still have a member of the junior house of Solomon on the throne of Judea; although of the Cushite house of David, they had gone over to the Elamites. We must remember that the two royal families were related in blood relationship owing to royal marriages; probably Jehoiakin was almost a pure Elamite.

I must now beg the reader not to forget that both the Cushites and the Elamites permeated every division of the empire,

Philistines and Israelites.

and may be regarded as two great parties, ranged under their respective flags. Precisely the same combination exists in England. The two races have become so blended together that they are hardly distinguishable; but the Tory and Radical flags point them out, and the thoughtful mind can as clearly define them, as when they met in conflict at the battle of Hastings.

In times of rebellion flags alone disclose the contending parties. I must submit there cannot be a shadow of doubt that Nebuchadnezzar marshalled his forces under the Elamite flag, and that Apries was contending with him under the Cushite flag. The two races are still in conflict which met at Siddim under the Cushite Abraham, and the Elamite Chedorlaomer, so there can be no question as to who were the contending powers. Priestly historians have, however, absolutely obscured them.

Genesis xiv, 3.

As the Elamite forces now garrisoned Jerusalem, the Cushites would retire to their strongholds on the sea coast; and we may be morally certain that the Pharaoh

Apries regained possession of Jerusalem as soon as the main army of Nebuchadnezzar had retired, for we find the forces of Nebuchadnezzar again in the field; Jehoiakin is deposed and Zedekiah his brother is placed on the throne:—

II. Chron. xxxvi. 13.

"And he also rebelled against King Nebuchadnezzar, who had made him swear by God; but he stiffened his neck and hardened his heart from turning unto the Lord God of Israel," which can only mean that he threw off his allegiance to the Elamite great king. The reader must notice that this glaringly exposes the two races; for if Zedekiah pulled down one flag he must put up another; and it is manifest that when he lowered the Elamite flag he adopted the colors of his chief, the Cushite Pharaoh Apries of the senior house of David.

Josephus, vol. i. 420.

We must now not fail to remember that when the Cushites under Apepi (*i.c.* Moses) occupied Canaan, the country became known as Philistia, and the Cushites as Philistines; but when, under the Elamite rule, the division of Philistia was broken up, and an Elamite petty king was appointed over the

I. Kings xii.

Philistines and Israelites.

province of Israel, the Philistine designation would drop out of use; hence the Cushites living in Judea, instead of being termed Philistines, would naturally be known as Jews. But as the two great races permeated Judea it becomes obvious that there were two races of Jews in Judea, viz.: the Philistine or Cushite Jews and the Elamite Jews of the tribe of Judah. It stands to reason then, when Zedekiah rebelled against the great Elamite king Nebuchadnezzar, he ran up the Philistine or Cushite flag over Jerusalem.

CHAPTER VIII.

II. Chron. xxxvi. 12.

WE learn from the Biblical narratives that Zedekiah humbled not himself before Jeremiah; it becomes then evident that Jeremiah was a representative of the Elamite Great King.

Jeremiah xx. 2.

Jeremiah was thundering his anathemas against the Jewish king; and the priestly writers inform us that Zedekiah "put him in the stocks, that were in the high gate of Benjamin." We must view this as a subtle combination in their design to degrade Jeremiah, and obscure his high position. It is more than probable that Jeremiah was the general-in-chief of Nebuchadnezzar's forces, and certainly a prince of the house of Elam.

We must bear in mind that the Pharaoh Apries of the Cushite house of David (*i.e.* Hirhor) was now supreme in Egypt; it follows that the chief of the royal Ramesside

Philistines and Israelites.

Elamite family was out of power; he would be a powerful and distinguished personage, and the conspicuous rival of the reigning Cushite Pharaoh.

It has by no means been clearly defined who the prophets, of the priestly writers, represented; but as we find them invariably associated with the party in opposition, might we not surmise that they were the leaders of the opposition party.

I have ventured to conjecture that the prophet Isaiah was the deposed Elamite Pharaoh known to us as Usargon. He was clearly the leader of the opposition, and there are grounds for supposing that he eventually succeeded to the throne of Elam.

We now find Jeremiah in a similar position, and I shall point out that he succeeded Apries as the Pharaoh of Egypt. This is practically confirmed, for we find that Zedekiah opens negociations with him when Jerusalem is besieged, and inquires if Nebuchadnezzar cannot be induced to raise the siege. Jeremiah tells him that the only policy he can adopt is to give up the town, and says: "He that abideth in this city

Jeremiah xxi. 9.

shall die by the sword: but he that goeth out, and falleth to the Chaldeans that besiege you, he shall live." This is clearly the ultimatum of the Great Elamite King. We can conclude that when Zedekiah defied the power of Elam he placed himself under the protection of the Cushite Pharaoh Apries, his chief; so that we are not surprised to find that the Pharaoh's forces appear on the scene and raise the siege: "And it came to pass, that when the army of the Chaldeans [Elamites] was broken up from Jerusalem for fear of the Pharaoh's army, then Jeremiah went forth out of Jerusalem to go into the land of Benjamin." This skilfully leads us to infer that Jeremiah and Zedekiah were of the same race and party, and subtly obscures the two belligerents. Might we not, under the circumstances, surmise that instead of Jeremiah going "into the land of Benjamin," he withdrew the Elamite forces "into the land of Babylon"? It is more than probable that the Cushite Pharaoh Apries followed up his victory, and expelled the Elamite troops from Western Asia?

Jeremiah xxxvii. 11.

Philistines and Israelites.

The Elamite forces some few years after again appear on the scene, led by Jeremiah, which certainly indicates that the Cushites were dominant. Jerusalem is closely besieged and fresh negotiations take place. "Then said Jeremiah unto Zedekiah; if thou wilt go forth unto the King of Babylon, thy soul shall live, but if thou wilt not go forth, then shall this city be given into the hands of the Chaldeans. And Zedekiah the king said unto Jeremiah, *I am afraid of the Jews* that are fallen to the Chaldeans, lest they deliver me into their hand, and they mock me. But Jeremiah said, they shall not deliver thee."

Jeremiah xxxviii. 17.

I present this record as one of the finest combinations in the Biblical plot; it is framed with a subtle alliance with truth, and still conveys an absolutely false impression.

Let me remind the reader that it is the design of the writers to obscure the great Cushite and Elamite races which have been rivals for empire since we were first introduced to them. But when we find it recorded that Zedekiah, the King of the

Jews, says he is afraid of the Jews, we become absolutely confounded. A moment's reflection will enable us to detect the craft of the record.

Zedekiah had rebelled against the Great King, and was now flying the Cushite Jewish flag; he was, therefore, naturally afraid of the Elamite Jews of the tribe of Judah; this is abundantly manifest, for Jeremiah assures him that the Elamite Jews will not revolt. The two rival races are therefore vividly before us. Let us tear the bandages from our eyes, and calmly view the situation. We shall then detect who are the two rival powers; and that it is not a conflict alone between Zedekiah, the petty king of Judea, and Jeremiah, the petty king of Israel, but the old, old struggle for supremacy in the empire between the Hamitic and Semitic races.

The Pharaoh Apries, now reigning in Egypt, represents the ancient line of Cushite kings of the house of Abraham; and Nebuchadnezzar personates the ancient line of the house of Chedorlaomer, or perhaps Menes. The siege of Jerusalem only dis-

Philistines and Israelites.

closes the old conflict for empire between these two rival houses. The Elamites, it is true, occupied Chaldea, but that does not transform them into Chaldeans, except as a territorial designation. Let us then understand they were still Elamites, and it is a gross perversion of history to allude to them as Chaldeans. We must, therefore, recognise that it was the Elamites who were besieging Jerusalem, and the Cushites were defending it.

The positions of the two belligerent forces are thus plainly indicated. The Cushite Philistine Jews held Jerusalem and their strongholds on the sea coast; and as the Pharaoh Apries was still absolute master of Egypt, the flag of Cush would float over every fortress from Jerusalem to Ethiopia. The Elamites dominated all Asia, north of Jerusalem; thus Judea and Israel were the two buffer provinces.

Let us now turn to the Biblical narratives and ascertain if this view is confirmed. Jeremiah himself admits us behind the scenes, and explains who Nebuchadnezzar was warring against in no uncertain words, for I contend that all the records are based on authentic facts: "The Lord of hosts, the God of Israel [*i.e.* Nebuchadnezzar], saith: Behold, I will punish the multitude of No, and Pharaoh, and Egypt, with their gods, and their kings, even Pharaoh, and all them that trust in him, and I will deliver them into the hand of Nebuchadezzar, king of Babylon." Here then the Cushite Pharaoh Apries is distinctly pointed out as one of the antagonists of Nebuchadnezzar.

"The word of the Lord that came to Jeremiah against the Philistines, thus saith the Lord: Behold waters rise up out of the north, and shall be an overflowing flood, and shall overflow the land, and all that is therein; because of the day that cometh to spoil all the Philistines, for the Lord will spoil the Philistines. Baldness is come upon Gaza: Ashkelon is cut off with the remnant of their valley."

Here, then, the Philistines are also clearly defined as antagonists of the Great King.

I must submit that this conclusively proves that the Elamite forces under Nebuchadnezzar were in conflict for supremacy in the empire with the Cushite forces of the Pharaoh Apries, and the Cushite forces only; for the Philistine Jews were only a section of the Cushite power.

"And in the ninth year of Zedekiah king of Judah, came Nebuchadnezzar king of Babylon and all his army against Jerusalem, and they besieged it." *Jeremiah xxxix.*

"And in the eleventh year of Zedekiah the city was broken up. And all the princes of the king of Babylon came in and sat in the middle gate. And when Zedekiah saw them, and all the men of war, then they fled. But the Chaldeans' army pursued after them and overtook Zedekiah in the plains of Jericho. And the King of Babylon slew the sons of Zedekiah before his eyes. Moreover he put out Zedekiah's eyes, and bound him with chains to carry him to Babylon. And the Chaldeans burned the king's house, and the houses of the people, with fire, and brake down the walls of Jerusalem. Then Nebuzar-adan the captain of the guard carried away captive into Babylon the remnant of the people that remained in the city, and *Jeremiah xxxix. 2.*

those that fell away, that fell to him, with the rest of the people that remained. But Nebuzar-adan left the poor of the people, which had nothing, in the land of Judah, and gave them vineyards and fields at the same time. Now Nebuchadnezzar gave charge concerning Jeremiah, saying, Take him, and look well to him, and do him no harm ; but do unto him even as he shall say unto thee. So the captain of the guard gave him victuals and a reward and let him go."

We are therefote led to infer that Jeremiah was a personage of very little consequence ; but the craft of the record will very soon appear; it absolutely obscures true history.

As I have pointed out that Jerusalem was defended by the Cushite Philistine Jews, it stands to reason that the Philistine Jews would be the prisoners taken into captivity. We are, however, adroitly led to believe that they were Israelites ; but as the term Israelite is only a territorial designation for the inhabitants of Israel, it becomes obvious that the Israelites had nothing whatever to do with the defence of Jerusalem; and as they were to a man supporting Nebuchadnezzar, it is clear they were not taken away as prisoners. The imposition of the priestly writers becomes then glaringly manifest.

We must remember that before Zedekiah threw off his allegiance to the great Elamite King, he had served under the Elamite flag; he would therefore control a considerable following of Elamite Jews of the tribe of Judah. And we have it recorded that Nebuchadnezzar not only massacred every member of Zedekiah's family he could lay his hands on, but he slew: "all the nobles of Judah," which unquestionably indicates that these Elamite Jews were supporting Zedekiah. *Jeremiah xxxix. 6*

It was only natural, when the Elamites came into power on the fall of Jerusalem, that all those who were banished by Zedekiah would flock into the country; and we find it recorded that "all the Jews that were in Moab, and among the Ammonites, and in Edom, and that were in all countries, heard that the King of Babylon had left a remnant of Judah, and that he had set over *Ibid. xl. 11.*

them Gedaliah; even all the Jews returned out of all places whither they had been driven and came to the land of Judah, to Gedaliah, unto Mispah, and gathered wine and summer fruits very much."

Here we have a very subtle combination, for we are insensibly led to confound the Elamite Jews of the tribe of Judah with the Cushite Philistine Jews; but let us reflect for one moment, and the imposition becomes glaringly exposed. Beyond a shadow of doubt the Philistine Jews who were defending Jerusalem had been defeated, and the Elamite Jews of the tribe of Judah were now paramount and gathering their rival's harvest. The prisoners taken captive by Nebuchadnezzar were therefore the Philistines, and those that escaped, retired to their strongholds on the sea coast.

The combinations in the priestly plot are simply superb, they are strictly framed on authentic facts, and yet convey an absolutely false impression; for we are insidiously led to imagine that Nebuchadnezzar was a Chaldean, and the Egyptians and the Philis-

Philistines and Israelites.

tines were two other foreign powers. I contend, however, I have conclusively proved that Nebuchadnezzar was the great Elamite king, and that he was warring against Apries, the Cushite Pharaoh of Egypt. I have also demonstrated that the Philistines were merely a section of the Cushite or Hyksos race, and it becomes obvious that the Israelites can only represent a section of the Elamite race. I submit that the Hamitic and Semitic races are undoubtedly disclosed.

Let there be no mistake; the records distinctly tell us that Nebuchadnezzar was at war with the Egyptians and the Philistines who held Jerusalem. This is a fact which does not admit of a doubt. It follows, then, that the prisoners taken away by Nebuchadnezzar from Jerusalem were Philistines and not Israelites. It therefore becomes obvious that the prisoners taken captive on the fall of Jerusalem, *said* to have been released by Cyrus, were not the chosen people of priestcraft, but their mortal enemies, the Philistines.

It will be noticed that the Philistines are

many times very pointedly alluded to as uncircumcised. I submit that this is one of the subtle distortions of priestcraft; for I contend that the Philistines did adopt this Cushite rite, and that the Israelites (*i.e.*, Elamites) did not. The Philistine Jewish prisoners of war, who returned from captivity under Zerubbabel, a prince of the Cushite house of David, were circumcised; which conclusively proves they were not Israelites (*i.e.*, Elamites). The writers clearly detected this, and they could only overcome the difficulty by insinuating that the Philistines were not circumcised; leading us insensibly to infer that the Israelites did practice this rite.

The reader will notice how skilfully this transforms the Elamite Jews, of the tribe of Judah, into the Cushite Jews who were taken prisoners at the fall of Jerusalem.

Herodotus xi. 104.

CHAPTER IX.

LET us still follow the events which succeeded the fall of Jerusalem.

A peace was probably concluded between the great Elamite King Nebuchadnezzar and the Cushite Pharaoh Apries, and the main armies of the Elamite King retire to Babylon. The Jews of the tribe of Judah flock into the country from all quarters and gather wine and summer fruits very much under their national king Gedaliah. We now learn that a conspiracy is detected, and Gedaliah is warned that Ishmael, one of the surviving princes of the house of Zedekiah, had threatened to slay him; but Gedaliah refused to believe it :—" Then Johanan spake to Gedaliah in Mizpah secretly, saying, Let me go, I pray thee, and I will slay Ishmael: wherefore should he slay thee, that all the Jews which are gathered unto thee should be scattered, and the remnant in

Jeremiah xl. 14.

Philistines and Israelites.

Judah perish?" There can be no doubt that the Jews here referred to represent the Elamite Jews of the tribe of Judah, who were reaping the rewards accruing to them, owing to the fall of Jerusalem. It, therefore, becomes glaringly apparent that the Jews of the tribe of Judah were not the Philistine Jews who defended Jerusalem, so we have the two races of Jews plainly before us.

The Philistine Jews had undoubtedly retired to their strongholds on the sea coast; and Ishmael, a prince of the house of Zedekiah, makes a raid into the province of Israel, murders Gedaliah, and a general massacre takes place in Mizpah:—"Now the pit wherein Ishmael had cast all the dead bodies of the men whom he had slain because of Gedaliah, was it which Asa the king had made for fear of Baasha king of Israel: and Ishmael filled it with them that were slain."

Jeremiah xli. 9.

The Cushite revenge was a savage one; but I only mention it as an instance to show what a deadly hatred must have existed between the two rival races.

"Then Ishmael carried away captive all the residue of the people that were in Mizpah, even the king's daughters [Gedaliah's], and all the people that remained in Mizpah." The Elamite forces pursue him, and as an engagement is recorded to have taken place at Gibeon, it becomes evident that Ishmael was retreating to his strongholds on the sea coast. *Jeremiah xli. 12.*

The Elamites appear to have succeeded in recovering their captives and their king Gedaliah's daughters, but perhaps thinking that discretion was the better part of valour, they cleared out of Judea as fast as they could and retreated to Egypt :—"And all the people, both small and great, and the captains of the armies arose and came to Egypt." Are we not forced to conclude that the Cushite Philistines, under Ishmael, had defeated the Elamite army of occupation and had driven them out of the country? The excuse given in the Biblical narratives why the Israelites under Jeremiah escaped to Egypt is singularly ingenious: "Because of the Chaldeans, for they were afraid of them, because Ishmael had *II. Kings xxv. 26.*   *Jeremiah xli. 18.*

slain Gedaliah, whom the king of Babylon made governor in the land." The reader will notice that this record insensibly leads us to believe that Nebuchadnezzar was warring against the Israelites.

That the Israelites felt themselves under the greatest obligations to Nebuchadnezzar is abundantly manifest, for Baruch, one of Jeremiah's priests, tells them: "To pray for the life of Nebuchadnezzar, and for the life of Balthasar his son, that their days may be on the earth as the days of Heaven." This is not a prayer that would suggest itself to the Philistine Jews, who had just been signally defeated, whose principal families had been taken into captivity, whose king had been mutilated, whose royal family had been massacred, and whose royal city had been sacked. The Cushites never offered up such a prayer for Nebuchadnezzar.

It has been the aim of the priestly writers and all their commentators to lead us to believe that the Israelites were taken into captivity at the fall of Jerusalem. In fact much of the framework of their narratives rests upon this. It is, however, obvious

Baruch i. 11.

Ezra ii. 1.

Philistines and Israelites.

that the prisoners taken captive by Nebuchadnezzar were the Philistine Jews who were defending the fortress under their petty king Zedekiah.

Fortunately the records are based upon authentic documents, and we can readily trace the two conflicting races; for we find it recorded that Nebuchadnezzar not only slew Zedekiah's sons, but *the nobles of Judah*, which unquestionably refers to the Elamite Jews of the tribe of Judah, who had ranked themselves under the Cushite flag. Here then the two races are distinctly exposed.

Jeremiah xxxix. 6.

It is again recorded that:—"In the three and twentieth year of Nebuchadnezzar the Captain of the Guard carried away captive of the Jews seven hundred forty and five persons: all the persons were four thousand and six hundred."

Jeremiah lii. 30.

Here again the two parties are palpably defined; hence we can conclude that 745 Elamite Jews, who were loyal to Zedekiah, and 3,855 Philistine Jews, were all the prisoners taken into captivity on the fall of Jerusalem. It is, however, the prominent aim of the priestly writers to lead us to infer that a vast number of Israelites, their God protected race, were taken away to Babylon as prisoners on the fall of Jerusalem, and that their families remained in exile nearly a century, until released by Cyrus, who is alluded to as a Persian and a worshipper of the one true God, which led him to befriend God's chosen people.

Ezra ii.

This view is already proved, and admitted, to be a delusion.

Fresh Lights from the Monuments, Prof. Sayce, 141.

There can be no doubt that the garbled records have tended to confuse us; but if we use our common sense a moment's reflection must convince us who the prisoners were who were taken into captivity by Nebuchadnezzar. Need I point to the Cushite forces serving under the Pharaoh Apries; they had probably been recruited from every province in the empire between Carchemish and Ethiopia.

I express a hope that I have made myself understood; but the priestly plot is full of marvellous combinations.

I may have fallen into some pitfalls, but confidently rely on scholars to give me a helping hand. I submit, however, I have proved beyond a shadow of doubt that the Israelites were not taken into captivity on the fall of Jerusalem, and the design of the writers mainly rests upon this delusion.

Perhaps priestcraft has secured a commanding position more through a claim of foresight than by any other method; for a prophecy of some startling event carries with it a conviction of divine inspiration.

I need not notice how easily compilers of history could insert predictions of events, after they had occurred, but they sometimes admit us behind the scenes. As an example I will recall the so-called prophet Daniel. A prophecy of Isaiah clearly points him out as a prince of the Cushite house of David.

Hezekiah is in trouble: "And Isaiah said unto Hezekiah:—Behold the days come, that all that is in thine house shall be carried into Babylon, and of thy sons that shall issue from thee, they shall be eunuchs in the palace of the king of Babylon." *II. Kings xx. 16.*

If the reader will turn to the Book of Daniel, it will be found this prophecy was fulfilled to the letter; and we find Daniel *Daniel i. 3.*

Philistines and Israelites.

a prince of the house of David, occupying a position in Babylon the most degrading it is possible for the western mind to realise; and we must understand his misfortune had been brought upon him through Jeremiah the Elamite; how bitter, then, must have been the hatred existing between Daniel and Jeremiah; yet we find their two books bound together in our Bible, and we are expected to derive instruction and religious consolation from both.

We may, however, assure ourselves that the whole story is pure fiction, only inserted to obscure the true position of Daniel, who was a royal prince of the Cushite house of David, and eventually succeeded to the throne under the name of Nabonidus.

This materially confirms my conjecture that the Prophets represented the leaders of the two races when out of power.

Upon a prediction of Jeremiah, who was certainly a Pharaoh of Egypt, the Roman Church founded its power to depose, with bell and book, King Henry the Eighth of England. This Bull of Pope Paul III. is so instructive, I venture to give some short extracts from it:—

"SENTENCE OF POPE PAUL III. AGAINST HENRY VIII.

"Condemnation and Excommunication of Henry VIII., King of England, and his Abettors and Accomplices, with the addition of other punishments.

"Paul, Bishop, servant of the servants of God, in perpetual remembrance of this matter.

"We, although unworthy, the vice-gerent on earth of Him who, unchangeable and eternal, governs all things, and placed in the seat of justice, according also to the prediction of the *Prophet Jeremiah* in these words: *Behold I have appointed thee over nations and kingdoms, that thou mayest pull up and destroy, build and plant; the chief over all the kings of the universe, and all peoples obtaining dominion.* Wherefore—after mature deliberation upon these matters with our venerable brothers the Cardinals —require in the Lord that King Henry entirely abstain from the aforesaid errors

C. H. Collette, Queen Elizabeth and the Penal Laws, Appendix A, 167.

Jeremiah i. 10.

and revoke, declare void, and annul the aforesaid constitutions and laws, as in fact he made them, and that he entirely abstain from compelling his subjects to keep them. Otherwise if King Henry and his abettors, adherents, advisers and followers shall not effectually obey the exhortations and requisitions of this kind, we excommunicate King Henry, his abettors, adherents, advisers and followers, by Apostolic authority, and pronounce that King Henry himself has incurred the penalty of deprivation of his kingdom and aforesaid dominion; and if in the meantime he shall die, we by our aforesaid authority and plenary power do declare and decree that he be deprived of ecclesiastical sepulture ; *and we strike them with the sword of anathema, malediction and eternal damnation.* And we absolve and altogether set free from the aforesaid king or his accomplices, and from the oath of allegiance, vassalage, and all obedience to the king, and other the parties aforesaid the magistrates, judges, constables, guardians, and officers of King Henry himself, and of his kingdom, and of all other his dominions.

Philistines and Israelites.

These nevertheless we command, under penalty of excommunication, entirely to abstain from obeying the same King Henry and his officers. We by the same authority do will and decree, that King Henry and his accomplices be from that time infamous and not permitted to give evidence. We warn all the faithfull in Christ to shun the aforesaid excommunicated, accursed, and condemned persons. Moreover we in like manner exhort and require the aforesaid princes, and all others even serving in the pay of the faithful in Christ, and other persons whomsoever, both by land and sea, who have men under arms, *that they rise in arms against King Henry*, his accomplices, and followers aforesaid, and that they persecute them, and every of them, and force and compel them to return to the unity of the Church, and obedience of the aforesaid See.

"Given at Rome at St. Mark in the year of our Lord 1535."

But what gave rise to no little surprise, King Henry retained the Papal revenues, which were then the only veritable bones in contention. It was the commencement of a great rebellion; and very shortly after the Teutonic race (probably Japhetic) threw off its allegiance to the house of Elam (*i.e.* the Pope). This has been ingeniously characterized as a religious reformation, which very neatly obscures a momentous racial revolution.

The Times, March 12th 1892

"Fifty years ago most English readers believed that they knew all about the foundation and authorship of the Old Testament. They supposed that Moses wrote the Pentateuch, that Joshua recorded the conquest of Canaan, that Samuel composed Judges and Ruth, that David wrote all the Psalms, and that the prophets themselves committed their own prophecies to writing. It was a simple and satisfactory theory as long as it remained unquestioned; but it was one that would not bear a moment's serious examination."

When we find the hightest authorities agree that neither Jeremiah nor any of the would-be prophets wrote the books ascribed to them, may we not conclude that the narratives were only compiled, in their present form, to further the aims of priestcraft, and does not the Bull of Pope Paul III. indicate the power the priests acquired through them, and the motives which dictated them?

As I contend that the Biblical records are invariably based upon authentic facts, it is more than probable that Jeremiah's so-called prediction, quoted by Pope Paul III., was the formal edict of Nebuchadnezzar appointing Jeremiah as the Pharaoh of Egypt. *Jeremiah i. 9.*

When the priestly design is detected, and we can assure ourselves that "the Lord," as used in the narratives, does not apply to the Almighty but to the Great King, true history becomes revealed.

The Tel-el-Amarna tablets clearly prove that the Pharaohs were recognised as deities, and the official despatches were addressed to the king as "My Lord, my God, my Sun God, who is from heaven," it follows that the edict of the Great King would be referred to as "the word of the Lord." *Jeremiah xliv. 1.*

Thus when we have it recorded that "the word of the Lord came to Jeremiah concerning all the Jews which dwell in the land of Egypt," we can only conclude that it was an edict from Nebuchadnezzar the Great King to his vassal Jeremiah [*i.e.*, Aahmes] the Pharaoh of Egypt.

I trust the reader will pardon my digression; but let us return to the retreat of the Elamites to Egypt after their defeat by the Cushite Prince Ishmael of the house of David; it is certainly authentic and discloses true history.

There can be no doubt that the Elamite troops would not have escaped to Egypt had Egypt been still in the possession of the Cushite Pharaoh Apries.

Fresh Lights from the Ancient Monuments, 132.

We are indebted to Professor Sayce for enabling us to clear up this difficulty. He tells us: "Records of Nebuchadnezzar's building operations exist in plenty, but of his annals only a small fragment has as yet been discovered. This however contains an allusion to his campaign in Egypt of which Jeremiah and Ezekiel prophesied, and which an over-hasty criticism has

Philistines and Israelites.

denied. The campaign, we learn, took place in the thirty-seventh year of his reign. Other references to it have been detected on the Egyptian monuments, and we gather from these that the Babylonian [Elamite] army swept the whole of the northern part of Egypt, and penetrated as far south as Assouan, from whence they were forced to retreat by the Egyptian [Cushite] general Hor. Amasis was at this time king of Egypt, having dethroned and murdered Apries, the Pharaoh Hophra of the Bible, whose miserable end had been foretold by Jeremiah (xliv. 30)."

Thus it becomes clear that the raid of Ishmael into the province of Israel occurred after the conquest of Egypt by Nebuchadnezzar.

The great Elamite king would now rule over the entire empire extending from Babylon to Thebes.

The Cushite power has fallen, and the Pharaoh Apries of the house of David (*i.e.* Hirhor) has been murdered. A general revolution must have taken place, and the Elamite house of Aahmes is once more

Philistines and Israelites.

triumphant. They had been eating the bread of subjection since Sabakah of the house of David (*i.e.* Hirhor) had wrested the prize out of their hands—a period of some hundred and fifty years.

CHAPTER X.

As we are told that the Cushite Pharaoh Apries has been murdered, an event which had been "foretold by Jeremiah," let us inquire who succeeded him on the throne of Egypt.

We are aware that Nebuchadnezzar had secured dominion over the entire empire from Elam to Thebes; so it becomes glaringly apparent that the great Elamite King had deposed Apries the Cushite Pharaoh; and we must distinctly bear in mind that Apries, before his deposition, was the greatest monarch in the world; for I have pointed out that he ruled from Nineveh to Ethiopia; hence a mighty revolution is disclosed. The Cushite power had fallen not alone in Egypt but over the entire Empire. The inscriptions inform us that his name was Uahabra; the Biblical writers refer to him as Hophra, and other historians term him Apries. This does not suggest the work of honest historians.

We learn from the inscriptions that Apries was succeeded by a Pharaoh of the name of Aahmes; historians, however, refer to him under the name of Amasis, which again suggests suspicion. We are, therefore, led to pause and inquire who this Pharaoh Aahmes could have been. As to his name there can be no mistake; it is precisely similar to that of Aahmes, an ancestor of Seti, and the founder of the great Elamite XVIIIth Egyptian dynasty; from which we must conclude he was of the same royal family; hence, an Elamite prince.

Nebuchadnezzar, the Great Elamite King, had undoubtedly deposed all the Cushite petty kings from Nineveh to Jerusalem.

The defeat of the Pharaoh Apries was his final conquest, for it placed him in absolute command of the entire empire. It was, therefore, the crowning event of his campaign. As we find this has been adroitly concealed by all historians, a vast conspiracy is disclosed, and we are forced

Philistines and Israelites.

to the conclusion that every historical record we possess has been garbled and distorted. Fortunately they have only been garbled, and if we eliminate the distortions true history is disclosed.

Owing to the discovery of inscriptions beyond the control of priestcraft, we are absolutely certain that Nebuchadnezzar invaded Western Asia and Egypt, and secured dominion from Babylon to Thebes. It follows he must have deposed some other power. I submit that I have conclusively proved that this power was represented by the flag of Cush, under Apries of the Cushite house of Abraham.

We must therefore understand that the Great Elamite King Nebuchadnezzar had vanquished his rivals the Cushites. Let us then look round and endeavour to trace who Nebuchadnezzar would place on the throne of Egypt; and we naturally turn to the conspicuous characters serving under his banner during his great campaign. There is only one prominent personage before us; need I point to Jeremiah? We can now detect why he did not accept the petty throne of Judea, taken by Gedaliah.

It was vital to the priestly design that this should be concealed; but when I assert that Aahmes, who succeeded the deposed Cushite Pharaoh Apries, represents Jeremiah, it is no rash conjecture; for we find Jeremiah speaking with an authority in Egypt which none but the Pharaoh could assume.

Jeremiah xliv. to li.

I will now point out that the Biblical narratives have not been the only vehicles adopted for the purpose of misrepresenting history.

The historian Herodotus, commonly known as the father of history, which suggests that general opinion ranks him before the Biblical historians, is supposed to have compiled his history about 450 B.C. only some hundred and forty years after the fall of Jerusalem and the rise of the Elamite power under Nebuchadnezzar, and as he is generally credited as an honest historian we should naturally expect to find a faithful record of all events connected with this great revolution; but, strange to relate, the power

Philistines and Israelites.

led by Nebuchadnezzar which secured him dominion over the entire empire from Babylon to Thebes is not once most distantly alluded to. A long rambling account is given of the Pharaohs of the XXVIth dynasty, but they are presented to us as only engaged in wars with Greeks and other maritime nations. The conquest of Egypt by Nebuchadnezzar is unnoticed.

The Pharaoh Apries is said to have been dethroned by some factions among the Egyptians, and Amasis (*i.e.* Aahmes), who succeeded him, is pointed out as a private person of no illustrious family. Amasis is said to have been, even when a private person, fond of drinking and jesting, and by no means inclined to serious business, and when the means failed him for drinking and indulging himself he used to go about pilfering.

All this is absolutely false, and I proclaim it as the forgery of arrant impostors. Its object is obvious; Aahmes, the Elamite Pharaoh who succeeded the Cushite Pharaoh Apries, must not be recognised as "Jeremiah."

I have pointed out that the great scholar Josephus, in a controversy he had with Apion concerning the origin of the Jews, asserts that the Jews were the old lords of Egypt [the Hyksos], who, after many centuries of glorious dominion, at length quitted it under an honourable convention, and the guidance of Moses (*i.e.* Apepi) long before the supposed date of an exodus of leprous outcasts under an apostate Egyptian priest, Osarsiph (*i.e.* Amenhotep III).

Bunsen's Egypt, vol. i. 198.

It becomes obvious that this well-known scholar Josephus cannot be the Flavius Josephus, who gives us a totally different version of the origin of the Jews; or else his history has been garbled and distorted in a similar manner to that of Herodotus, which is more than probable.

I have ventured to assert, when Zedekiah rebelled against the great Elamite King Nebuchadnezzar, that he hoisted the Cushite flag of the Pharaoh Apries over Jerusalem.

If we turn to the spurious history of Josephus we shall find the familiar combination is adopted for obscuring the two great Hamitic and Semitic races, by allud-

Philistines and Israelites.

ing to them under their territorial designations as Egyptians and Babylonians.

Nebuchadnezzar, the great King of Elam, had captured Carchemish from the Cushite Pharaoh Apries; following up his victory he had invaded Western Asia, driving the Cushite forces before him till they made a stand in their strong fortress of Jerusalem. If we recognise that the Egyptian power under the Pharaoh Apries represents the Cushite flag, and Nebuchadnezzar was warring against it, under the Elamite flag, the two great races are clearly defined struggling for supremacy in the empire.

It has been the aim of the priestly writers to lead us to infer that Zedekiah was an independent monarch; but let us remember he was a lineal descendant of the house of Solomon, who had gone over to the Elamites; and as the Pharoah Apries was a descendant of the senior branch of the Cushite house of David (*i.e.* Hirhor), it was only natural that Zedekiah, when he threw off his allegiance to the Great King, would run up the Cushite flag of his chief the Pharaoh of Egypt. This is solidly confirmed by Josephus, for although distorted like the Biblical narratives, his facts are based upon authentic records.

The priestly writers in their version of the siege of Jerusalem entirely obscure the Egyptian (*i.e.* Cushite) power; but Josephus admits us behind the scenes:— "Now when Zedekiah preserved the league of mutual assistance he had made with the Babylonians [*i.e.* Elamites] for eight years he broke it, and revolted *to the Egyptians* [*i.e.* Cushites]. When the King of Babylon knew this he made war against him, and took his fortified towns, and came to the city of Jerusalem itself to besiege it; but when the King of Egypt heard what circumstances Zedekiah, his ally, was in, he took a great army with him and came into Judea, as if he would raise the seige; upon which the King of Babylon departed from Jerusalem and met the Egyptians, and joined battle with them and beat them, and when he had put them to flight he pursued them, and drove them out of all Syria."

But when we find that Zedekiah still held Jerusalem, we may reasonably surmise that,

Josephus, vol. i. 420.

Philistines and Israelites.

instead of Nebuchadnezzar driving the Cushites out of all Syria, the Cushite Pharaoh Apries drove the Elamite forces out of all Syria. This is practically confirmed, for we find the Great King has again to invade the country shortly after, when he sacks Jerusalem and takes Zedekiah and many other nobles as prisoners to Babylon.

Josephus again admits us behind the scenes in a very instructive record :—" And now, because we have enumerated the succession of the kings, and who they were, and how long they reigned, I think it necessary to set down the names of the high priests, and who they were that succeeded one another in the high priesthood under the kings. The first high priest then at the temple which Solomon built, was Zadoc ; after him his son Achimas ; after Achimas was Asarias ; then follow Joram, Issus, Axioramas, Phideas, Sudeas, Juelus, Jotham, Urias, Nerias, Odeas, Sallumus, Elcias Azarias, Sareas and Josedek, who was carried captive to Babylon. All these received the high priesthood by succession, the sons from their father."

Josephus, vol. i. 425.

As we must suppose that these were the high priests of the temple in Jerusalem, we are led to inquire why they have been obscured in the Biblical narratives. But as I have conclusively proved that David, who founded this temple, was the Pharaoh Hirhor the high priest of Amen, we may be morally certain that the high priests named by Josephus were the high priests of Amen. If this is not the case perhaps students will explain who these high priests were.

I. Chron. xxix. 2.

Let us now return to the Pharaoh Aahmes who succeeded the deposed Cushite Pharaoh Apries. Aahmes is no unknown character; he was placed on the throne by Nebuchadnezzar and was his vassal. His name is recorded on the Egyptian cartouches, and it is identical with the Aahmes of the XVIIIth Elamite Egyptian dynasty; and we find him conspicuously engaged in the burial of an Apis bull.

Dr. Brugsch gives us a full translation of the tablet recording it, to which I must refer the reader for details. We gather it was a gorgeous pageant: "They were prepared more splendidly than ever before, for

Brugsch, vol. ii. 297.

Philistines and Israelites.

his majesty had loved the living Apis better than all the other kings. This is what was done for him by Aahmes Si-Neit who bestows pure life for ever."

The granite sarcophagus of this bull stands to this day *in situ*, in the Serapeum; and it exposes the gross fraud imposed upon us in the pages of Herodotus, who never could have recited such arrant nonsense. It has clearly been interpolated for the purpose of obscuring Jeremiah as the Pharaoh of Egypt, just as Abraham, Moses, and David have been foisted on us as simple shepherds. It was vital to the priestly design that their characters should be stripped of worldly power, and appear only as vicegerents of the Almighty.

We must now understand that the Great King Nebuchadnezzar had subjugated Egypt, and deposed the Pharaoh Apries; it was not, however, a decisive blow which crushed the Cushite power.

We have it recorded in the Biblical narratives that the Cushite prince Ishmael, of the seed royal of the house of David, made a raid from his strongholds and ex-

See Herodotus, iii. 27.

Jeremiah xli.

pelled the Elamites from Judea ; and as the Elamites retreated to Egypt, Egypt must certainly at this time have been in possession of the Elamite Pharaoh Aahmes (*i.e.* Jeremiah) ; and, as we gather from the inscriptions that Aahmes was succeeded by a Pharaoh of the name of Psamethik ; and we know that Psamethik was a Cushite of the house of David (*i.e.* Hirhor), it becomes manifest that another revolution had taken place ; and when we learn that Ishmael succeeded Zedekiah as leader of the Cushites, we may reasonably surmise that Ishmael represents Psamethik III. who we find on the throne of Egypt.

Jeremiah xli. 1.

The Elamite Pharaoh, Aahmes (*i.e.* Jeremiah), placed on the throne by Nebuchadnezzar, must therefore have been deposed ; and this, to a certain extent, is confirmed, for we find Jeremiah predicting the fall of Babylon ; which certainly indicates that a revolution had occurred and Babylon had passed under the rule of a rival power. It follows that the Cushites would be again supreme.

Professor Sayce tells us that Nebuchadnezzar had a long reign of nearly forty-three years. His son and successor, Evil Merodach, lived hardly three years after his accession, and then was murdered by his brother-in-law, Nergal-Sharezer, who seized the crown. His son who succeeded him was a mere boy, and was murdered after a brief reign of four months. The throne was then usurped by Nabonidus *who does not seem to have belonged to the royal family.* The Professor touches upon this very lightly; but must we not conclude that the Elamite power has fallen? and, as we find the Cushite Pharaoh Psamethik still all-powerful in Egypt, might we not hazard a conjecture that Nabonidus represented the Cushite party? We must remember that there are only two competing powers in the Empire; hence, if the Elamite party has been overthrown, there is no other power to take its place but the Cushite; this becomes certainly confirmed when we find them masters of Egypt.

I therefore submit there can be no doubt that Nabonidus secured his position as Great King under the Cushite flag; and we may

See Fresh Light from the Monuments, 133.

confidently conclude that the Cushites are again in power from Babylon to Ethiopia.

The Professor goes on to tell us that "Nabonidus reigned for seventeen years," when another great revolution is disclosed, which historians have carefully obscured; and, as Professor Sayce adds, that Nabonidus witnessed the rise of a *new power* in the east, another element of confusion is anticipated. We come, then, to the rise of the Persian power under Cyrus; but as I have conclusively proved that there were only two races struggling for supremacy in the empire, it stands to reason, if my position is a tenable one, that Cyrus must have acquired dominion under the Elamite flag. It is true he is designated as a Persian by the Biblical writers and all historians; but may we not detect the old subtle combination in the plot. The Elamites have now moved their seat of government to the territorial division of Persia; and the writers, in order to obscure their race, adroitly refer to them by their territorial designation as Persians. Need I point out again that territorial designations give no

Philistines and Israelites.

indication of race ; and, as it was vital to the priestly design that the Elamites should be obscured, they are, with consumate craft, alluded to as Persians.

The reader is doubtless losing patience, and will imagine I am following a phantom Elamite flag. I readily admit that my argument stands or falls on my being able to prove, beyond a shadow of doubt, that Cyrus, the would-be Persian, secured his dominion over the entire Eastern Empire under the Elamite flag. I may therefore be permitted to review my position.

As Abraham's race is adroitly concealed in the Biblical narratives, we are led to inquire who they were. As we find it recorded that father Ham's (*i.e.* Abraham's) eldest son, was Cush, we are led to presume that Abraham represented the Cushite or Hamitic race. But when it has been disclosed that Hirhor or Nisbindidi, an hereditary prince, King's son of Cush, and Pharaoh of Egypt, was no other than David, a lineal descendant of the seed of Abraham, our presumption is massively confirmed ; and it becomes an absolute certainty when

Philistines and Israelites.

Assyrian Eponymn Canon, 142.

we find that the Pharaoh Tirhakah of the house of Hirhor (*i.e.* David) is styled in the Assyrian inscriptions as King of Cush.

I must remind the reader that the fall of the XIIth Egyptian dynasty synchronises with the defeat of the Elamites by Abraham; when, therefore, the inscriptions disclose that a foreign race, obscured under the name of the Hyksos, came into power on the fall of the XIIth dynasty and exercised dominion during seven centuries; we can only conclude that the Hyksos represent the race of Abraham.

Although Seti claims all the Pharaohs of the XIIth dynasty as his ancestors, he passes over all the Hyksos Pharaohs, and claims Aahmes who deposed them. And, as I contend that Abraham represents the Cushite race which overthrew the Elamites, it follows that the XIIth dynasty represented the Elamites, and further that the so-called Hyksos were Cushites; and as we have traced these two rival races in constant conflict for supremacy ever since, that is from about 2200 B.C. to 600 B.C. a period of sixteen hundred years, and no other race has appeared on the scene, we can only conclude that the Persians were not another foreign race which had suddenly popped up, but the old Elamites masked under another name. The reader will notice that the two races have been concealed by the priestly historians with consummate skill under many different appellations; and probably my conception of history would not have obtained credence had it not been for a little tablet which has escaped destruction. But this precious little tablet proves, beyond a question of doubt, that Cyrus, the would-be Persian of the priestly historians, was the lineal descendant of a long line of Elamite Kings, and the Great King of Elam.

The reader will now detect that my position is absolutely confirmed; and, I boldly assert, that it shatters the priestly plot to its very foundation.

We are indebted to Professor Sayce for his translation of this remarkable tablet, and I must refer my readers to his interesting little work for all details. Cyrus explains very vividly who he was: " I am Cyrus, the king of legions, the great king, the powerful

Fresh Light from the Monuments, 139.

king, the King of Babylon, the King of Sumer and Accad, the king of the four Zones, the son of Kambyses, the great king, the King of Elam ; the grandson of Cyrus the great king, the King of Elam ; the great-grandson of Teispes, the great king, the King of Elam ; of the ancient seed royal, whose rule has been beloved by Bel and Nebo, whose sovereignty they cherished according to the goodness of their hearts."

There can be no doubt, then, that Cyrus was the great Elamite King, and every historian must have known it.

Cyrus goes on to inform us that "All the kings who dwell in the high places of all regions from the upper sea to the lower sea, who dwelt in the high places of the Kings of Phœnicia and Sutar, all of them brought their rich tribute, and in the midst of Babylon kissed my feet . . . . Accad, Marad, Zamban, Me-Turnat and Duran as far as the border of Kurdistan, the fortresses (which lie) upon the Tygris, wherein from of old were their seats ; I restored the Gods who dwelt within them to their places, and I enlarged (for them) seats that

Philistines and Israelites.

should be long enduring; all the peoples I assembled, and I restored their lands. And the Gods of Sumer and Accad whom Nabonidus, to the anger of the Lord of Gods (Merodach), had brought into Babylon, I settled in peace in their sanctuaries by the command of Merodach, the great lord."

It becomes then apparent that Cyrus the Elamite had subjugated Nabonidus the Cushite; and it proves very forcibly that the Cushite cult was different to that of the Elamites.

The Professor adds: "Such are the records which have risen up, as it were out of the tomb, to revolutionise all our previous conceptions of that part of ancient history with which they are concerned." With all due deference to the learned Professor, I assert that these records, not only revolutionise all our previous conceptions of history relating to Cyrus, but the whole history of the eastern empire; for all Cyrus' ancestors were mighty monarchs ruling over the entire empire from Elam to Thebes; and, when the Elamite flag did not control the empire, the Cushite flag took its place; and these two powers have been absolutely concealed by the priestly historians.

This precious tablet throws still more light upon the scene, for Cyrus gives us the names of his ancestors; we have therefore no longer to grope in the dark, nor can we be misled by the priestly writers.

Sydney Smith tells us that "Errors, to be dangerous, must have a great deal of truth mingled with them," thus, when we find records subtly based upon specious truth, which are calculated to convey a false impression, grave suspicion must rest on the authors.

The question under discussion vividly illustrates this. We find it recorded that Cyrus was a Persian, and it cannot be denied that historians were quite as justified in alluding to him as a Persian as they were in terming the Norman William an Englishman, thus the record is subtly allied with truth. As regards the Normans it was highly desirable for all parties that the Norman flag should be obscured; but no such reason can be suggested for dubbing Cyrus a Persian. We are therefore forced to the conclusion that Cyrus was so named for the sole purpose of obscuring the Elamite flag, leading us to believe he was the leader of a race, foreign to the Elamites, in race and religion.

Now that we have learnt from Cyrus' cylinder that he was the Great King of Elam, it becomes evident that his conquest of the empire was only another struggle for supremacy between the rival Semitic and Hamitic races.

Cyrus undoubtedly represented the house of Chedorlaomer the Great King of Elam, and the Pharaoh Psamethik represented the house of Abraham.

We are led to infer that Cyrus' religious sentiments induced him to favour a race presented to us as specially protected by the Almighty. This view is lovingly dwelt upon by commentors. Cyrus is alluded to as "an inspired prophet" (Isaiah xliv. 28), recognized in him "a shepherd" of the Lord, an "anointed" king, the Messiah, and the title seemed to later writers to invest him

Dictionary of the Bible, Cyrus.

with the dignity of being in some sense a type of Christ himself.

But when we discover from long lost contemporaneous inscriptions that Cyrus was the Great King of Elam and the successor of a long line of Great Kings of Elam, that he was a follower of the would-be false gods Merodach, Bel, and Nebo, and his son, Cambyses, was an adorer of the sacred Bull Apis, it becomes apparent that history has been egregiously distorted. But when we detect that it was vital to the priestly design that the great Semitic race which Cyrus represented should be obscured, we can only view the motives which dictated such fabrications with the gravest concern in the light they throw on all the other records.

If I have convinced the reader that Cyrus secured dominion over the eastern empire under the flag of Elam it follows that Nabonidus, the King of Babylon, and Psamethik, the Pharaoh of Egypt, whom he deposed and supplanted, must have been contending against him under another flag, and I submit I have conclusively proved that Psamethik was a lineal descendant of

Philistines and Israelites.

Hirhor (*i-e.* David), and as Hirhor styled himself as King of Cush, it is absolutely certain that Psamethik was flying the Cushite flag.

As I am only glancing over history I must leave it to unbiased students for further elucidation; but I will point out that, if Cyrus' tablet is authentic, there can be no doubt that history has been grossly distorted.

We know that Nebuchadnezzar wrested the dominion of Western Asia and Egypt out of the hands of the Pharaoh Apries, and that he placed Aahmes on the throne of Egypt under the Elamite flag.

Another revolution takes place. Psamethik III. deposes Aahmes in Egypt, and Nabonidus acquires dominion over the Asiatic Empire. It becomes evident, then, that Psamethik and Nabonidus, at this period, ruled over the entire Eastern Empire under the Cushite flag.

Josephus informs us that Daniel was a prince of the house of Zedekiah and was taken captive to Babylon, where he was known under the name of Baltasar. Jose-

Whiston's Josephus, Book x. Chap. x. 429.

phus also tells us that: "when Evil Merodach was dead, after a reign of eighteen years, Niglissar (Nergal-sharezer), his son, took the government and retained it forty years; and after him the succession in the kingdom came to his son, Labosordacus, who continued in it in all but nine months; and when he was dead it came to Baltasar, who by the Babylonians was called Naboandelus (Nabonidus). Against him did Cyrus, the king of Persia, and Darius, the king of Media, make war."

As we know that Daniel was a royal prince of the Cushite house of Zedekiah, we may infer that he was the lineal heir to the Cushite throne; and as I have pointed out that Nabonidus secured his kingdom under the flag of Cush, having deposed the dynasty of Nebuchadnezzar, we might surmise that Daniel and Nabonidus were identical personages; but when we learn from Josephus that both Daniel and Nabonidus were called Baltasar, we may be morally certain that Daniel and Nabonidus were one and the same king. Truth will out, however cleverly it may be concealed!

Whiston's Josephus, Book xi. 434.

Ibid. 434.

Ibid. 429. 434.

Philistines and Israelites.

Another revolution takes place. Cyrus deposes both Nabonidus and Psamethik and becomes absolute master of the whole Empire under the flag of Elam. But Cyrus tells us he was the Great King of Elam, the son of Kambyses the Great King of Elam, the grandson of Cyrus the Great King of Elam, the great grandson of Teispes the Great King of Elam; and as the great kings of Elam reigned over the entire Eastern Empire, Nebuchadnezzar must have been one of Cyrus' ancestors masked under another name, probably Cyrus I.

We may be certain that the so-called Nebuchadnezzar was supreme over the vast Eastern Empire, extending from Elam to Thebes. Where can we find an empire for Cyrus the Great King of Elam the grandfather of Cyrus the Great King of Elam, unless we recognise him in the mask of Nebuchadnezzar? The reader will notice that this is by no means the first mask we have lifted.

We naturally again turn to Herodotus, the honest historian and father of history; he also gives us a list of Cyrus' ancestors—

Deioces, Phraortes, Cyaxares, Astyages, Cyrus. This is probably quite correct; but why trace his descent through his mother's family?

It becomes, then, glaringly apparent that history has been systematically distorted, and we can only hope to gain an insight into true history from inscriptions beyond the control of priestcraft.

Professor Sayce now informs us that:— "The Empire of Cyrus was broken up after the death of his son Kambyses, and had to be reconquered by Darius, the son of Hystaspes, the real founder of the Persian Empire." The Professor would then have us believe that the Persians were still a foreign race, and that they did subjugate the Empire. But as I have proved that there were only two races, viz., the Cushite and the Elamites, contending for supremacy, I must still maintain that Darius was a great Elamite king and succeeded Cyrus under the Elamite flag.

It is true that Darius styles himself a Persian; but as I pointed out that Persia was under the rule of the Elamite Great King,

Cyrus, as well as Darius and all the Elamite great kings, could style themselves kings of Persia, precisely as the Norman William and his dynasty could style themselves kings of England, it is merely a territorial designation, and does not indicate race. But Dr. Brugsch gives us a translation of another precious tablet which proves beyond question that Darius was the Great Elamite King. This tablet introduces us to a certain Sutenrekh (*i.e.* king's grandson) named Uza-hor-en-pi-ris, a high priest of the Goddess Nit; and he tells us: "Now king Darius, may he live for ever! commanded me to go to Egypt, while he was in the land of Elam, for he also was the great Lord of all lands and a great King of Egypt." Hence it follows that Darius, who succeeded Cyrus, was also the great Elamite king. This is confirmed by Herodotus, for he informs us that Darius, the son of Hystaspes, was a lineal descendant of Cyrus.

When we have discovered that Cyrus did not represent a new race, but was the great King of Elam and the lineal descendant of a long and illustrious line of Elamite kings;

Brugsch, vol. ii. 305.

Herodotus, Polymnia, vi. 415.

it becomes manifest that all history has been garbled and distorted. We can, therefore, only conclude that before the rise of the Elamites under Cyrus, the Cushites under Nabonidus and Psamethik were paramount over the entire Eastern Empire; consequently the Cushite prisoners taken captive by Nebuchadnezzar on the fall of Jerusalem would all have been liberated. It follows, then, that the captives released by Cyrus must have been the prisoners he had himself taken during his victorious campaign against Nabonidus and Psamethik III. This is practically confirmed, for we find they returned under Zerubbabel, a prince of the Cushite house of David.

The seventy years captivity of the Israelites (*i.e.* Elamites) is obviously pure fiction. I will now give the reader a pause for reflection.

CHAPTER XI.

I HAVE taken it for granted, thus far, that our precious little tablet, disclosing Cyrus as an Elamite king, is authentic.

It is almost impossible to credit that all our historians and the Biblical writers could have been ignorant of a historical fact of such wide-world importance; we are, therefore, led to inquire whether the tablet is genuine. Mr. Albert Löwy, in an article which appeared in the "Scottish Review," April 1887, seems to convincingly prove that the much-talked of "Moabite stone" is a "fraudulent fabrication"; may not the Cyrus tablet be also spurious? We shall naturally turn to the father of history for information.

Herodotus was a Greek born in Asia Minor; he had devoted his life to study, and being a man of rank and wealth, he gathered his information by personally visit-

Biographie Universelle.

ing the seats of governments within the Eastern Empire; and on his return compiled his history, which he read before the Athenian Assembly in 444 B.C. Hence the rise of the Elamite power under Cyrus had only taken place some eighty years previously. We must, however, remember that the cylinder discloses that Cyrus was the son of Cambyses, a reigning Elamite emperor, who was descended from a long and glorious line of Elamite monarchs. His dynasty was still ruling from Elam to Thebes. Herodotus, then, must have been intimately acquainted with the whole political situation. It will, therefore, be interesting to study his narratives in connection with the birth and life of Cyrus.

Herodotus, Clio, 1—107.

He fortunately gives us the minutest details, and tells us that Astyages, a king of Media, had a daughter named Mundane; and having dreamed that her offspring would acquire dominion in the empire became exceedingly alarmed, and gave his daughter, when arrived at a marriageable age, to no one of the Medes who was worthy of her, through dread of the vision, but to a Persian

Philistines and Israelites.

named Cambyses, whom he found of good family and a peaceful disposition, deeming him far inferior to a Mede of moderate rank. He has another dream which confirms the first, so he sent to Persia for his daughter, who was then near her time of delivery; and upon her arrival he put her under a guard resolving to destroy whatever should be born of her; for the Magian interpreters had signified to him from his vision that the issue of his daughter would reign in his stead. We then have a long rambling account how that the king gave the child, as soon as it was born, to one of his servants with orders to murder it, and bury the body wherever he thought fit. The child, however, is saved by a subterfuge, and appears ten years after, playing in the village in which ox-stalls were, with boys of his own age, in the road The boys who were playing chose this reputed son of the herdsman for their king; and as one of them refused to obey the orders of Cyrus, he scourged the boy very severely. This leads to Astyages recognising Cyrus as his grandson. A long rigmarole follows to which I need

Philistines and Israelites.

not refer; it concludes by informing us that Cyrus eventually became the Persian King of all Asia, and not one word concerning the Elamite power.

It becomes, then, very apparent that such a conception of the political situation is absolutely inconsistent with the view revealed by King Cyrus's cylinder; and this cylinder is vouched for by Professor Sayce as an authentic document. I therefore assert, with every confidence, that the narratives attributed to Herodotus are interpolations, and the forgeries of rank impostors; and, as they cunningly support the priestly writers, we can easily detect the culprits. "We have been at their mercy," as Cardinal Newman tells us; and very little mercy have they shown us. We have only to glance over Herodotus to find it a tissue of fabrications, which craftily corroborate the priestly narratives; and this, forsooth, is our school text book.

Now that we know that Cyrus was the Great King of Elam, and a devoted follower of the Elamite worship, we may be certain that Cambyses, his son, followed the same cult.

A record is however inserted to lead us to believe he was a Persian, and a worshipper of the "true God." It was therefore necessary to conceal his adoration of the god Apis; and we are told: "When the priests brought Apis, Cambyses, like one almost out of his senses, drew a dagger, meaning to strike the belly of Apis, but hit the thigh; then falling into a fit of laughter he said to the priests: 'Ye blockheads, are there such gods as these, consisting of blood and flesh and sensible of steel? This truly is a god worthy of the Egyptians. But you shall not mock me with impunity.' Having thus spoken, he commanded those, whose business it was, to scourge the priests and to kill all the Egyptians whom they should find feasting. But Apis, being wounded in the thigh, lay and languished in the Temple; and at length, when he had died of his wound, the priests buried him without the knowledge of Cambyses. But Cambyses, as the Egyptians say, immediately became mad in consequence of this atrocity, though indeed he was not of sound mind before."

Herodotus, iii. 16.

Herodotus, iii. 29.

This record has been palpably inserted to

lead us to infer that Cambyses was of foreign origin, and in no way connected with the worship of the god Apis.

The flagrant imposition is exposed by the inscriptions: "According to an inscription, first found by me in Egypt but unfortunately much mutilated, this Apis was buried in the Serapeum in the fourth year of the king's reign. On the same stone we see Cambyses represented under his regal name, *in a kneeling posture, distinctly as a worshipper of the Apis-bull.* Underneath is a long inscription, of which I could only make out the first two lines: "Year 4, month Epiphi, under the reign (of King Cambyses), the bestower of life for ever, this God was carried to his burial in his place, which his majesty had already caused to be prepared for him." It follows, of undeniable necessity, that the Apis in question died, and was buried under the auspices of the Great King Cambyses himself.

When we recognise that Cambyses was neither a Persian nor the leader of a foreign race, but the son of Cyrus the Great King of Elam, and a lineal descendant of all the

Brugsch, vol. ii. 299.

Elamite Pharaohs, the imposition becomes glaringly exposed.

Let us steady our thoughts, and briefly review the political situation. Nebuchadnezzar, an undoubted ancestor of Cyrus the Great King of Elam, had wrested the empire out of the hands of the Cushite Pharaoh Apries and had placed Aahmes (*i.e.* Jeremiah) on the throne of Egypt as his vassal. *Josephus, vol. i. 428.*

Another revolution took place. Nabonidus, under the flag of Cush, deposed the dynasty of Nebuchadnezzar; and Psamethik III. replaced Aahmes on the throne of Egypt. Another revolution follows, when Cyrus, the Great King of Elam, invades the empire, deposes both Nabonidus and Psamethik, and places his son Cambyses on the throne of Egypt.

When we turn to Herodotus an entirely different historical review is presented to us. The fall of the Cushite Pharaoh Apries, and the rise of Nebuchadnezzar as ruler over the vast Eastern Empire, is not most distantly alluded to. The fall of Nebuchadnezzar's dynasty, and the rise of Na- *Herodotus, Book iii.*

bonidus and Psamethik over the same empire, receives no notice.

The fall of Nabonidus and Psamethik and the rise of Cyrus the Great King of Elam is so distorted that we are led to suppose Cyrus was a Persian, and the leader of a foreign race.

The Elamite Pharaoh Aahmes (*i.e.* Jeremiah) placed on the throne of Egypt by Nebuchadnezzar, is alluded to as Amasis, and Cambyses the son of Cyrus the Great King of Elam, is said to have been at war with him.

The Cushite Pharaoh Psamethik, who deposed the Elamite Pharaoh Aahmes, is said to have been his [Aahmes'] son and successor, and eventually was deposed by Cambyses.

The great struggle for supremacy between the house of Elam and the house of Cush, we are led to suppose, was a war between the Persians and the Egyptians.

The Cushites, whose empire Cyrus had overthrown, and whose forces had retired to their dominions in Ethiopia, are alluded to as Ethiopians; leading us to infer they were negroes.

Philistines and Israelites.

These records are all based on a substratum of truth, but they have been garbled and falsified with the view of supporting the priestly narratives. Can any other motive be possibly suggested?

It cannot be questioned that the Biblical writers, and all their commentators, distinctly lead us to believe that Cyrus was a Persian and the head of a new dynasty, foreign in race and religion.

The reader will notice the importance of this; for we have before us a gross imposition which cannot be cloaked, now Cyrus' cylinder has revealed him, not only as the Great King of Elam, but the lineal descendant of all the kings of Elam. He undoubtedly secured his throne as the lineal heir of the Elamite royal family, and followed the same religion as all his ancestors, and flew the same flag. He, therefore, had no connection whatever with a Persian religion or a Persian flag. The accession of Cyrus to power simply indicated that the Elamites had subjugated the Cushites; that is, the Semitic race had vanquished the Hamitic race.

It was vital to the priestly design that these two rival races should be obscured; hence we can readily detect why the Biblical writers and their commentators wish us to believe that Cyrus was a Persian. It obliterated the race of Elam. Now that we have discovered the imposition, and can be morally certain that Cyrus, the Great King of Elam, was a lineal descendant of Chedorlaomer, the Great King of Elam; we may also be certain that the religion practised by Chedorlaomer was the same religion as that followed by Cyrus; and this religion is absolutely ignored by the priestly writers.

We may also be absolutely certain that the religion practised by Cyrus, the Great King of Elam, was also followed by his dynasty, which reigned supreme over the Asiatic Empire till about 336 B.C., when it was overthrown by Alexander under the flag of Cush.

It becomes clear then that Cyrus was the chief of the great Semitic race and the lineal descendant of the former Great Kings of Elam, who had ruled, alternately with the

Philistines and Israelites.

Great Kings of Cush, over the Eastern Empire during thousands of years.

When, therefore, we turn to Herodotus, the familiar text book of our schooldays, and find his conception of history is significantly based on the assumption that Cyrus and his dynasty were the leaders of a foreign Persian race, and followed a peculiar form of Persian worship, we are irresistibly led to the conclusion that not alone Herodotus, but all our sources of historical information have been flagrantly distorted and garbled for the purpose of supporting a priestly design.

It is obvious that we can only hope to acquire reliable information from documents beyond the control of priestcraft; and I earnestly appeal to unbiased students to follow them up.

The true history of the world still lies buried under the sands of Egypt; let us take care we are no longer imposed on.

I must leave it for students to unravel the gross imposture, and pass on to more reliable history.

The Elamites are now in power under the dynasty of the Great Elamite King

Cyrus. The Cushite house of David is in the cold shade of opposition and watching their opportunity in Ethiopia.

The Elamite dynasty remained in power for more than a century, so the land must have enjoyed a long rest from war. As we have only been glancing at recurrent revolutions, periods of repose have been passed over, it is therefore quite refreshing to notice a peaceful interval.

It is well known to students that Psamethik I. of the house of David (*i. e.* Hirhor) was on the most friendly terms with the Lacedemonian Greeks. They were now a great power; we are, therefore, not surprised to find that the Cushite house of David was allied with them against the Elamites, who are now known as Persians. On the death of Darius II. a struggle for succession to the Elamite throne took place between Artaxerxes II. and his brother Cyrus, his name strikingly indicating that he was of the family of the Great Elamite King Cyrus. This war of succession gave the house of David their opportunity; and, as we find that a Pharaoh of the name of

Philistines and Israelites.

Amyrtæus ascends the throne of Egypt, we can only conclude that another revolution had taken place, and the Persian Elamite dynasty in Egypt has fallen. Amyrtæus reigned only some six years, when he was succeeded by Naifaurot, just at the moment when Sparta had declared war against the Persian Elamites; we might, therefore, gather that the Cushites were in close alliance with the Lacedemonians. This is strikingly confirmed, for we find it recorded that the Cushite Jews were of the same race as the Lacedemonians: "It is found in writing that the Lacedemonians and the Jews are brethren, and that they are of the stock of Abraham."

Brugsch, vol. ii. 335.

I. Maccabees, vii. 21.

The reader will notice, if this record can be relied upon, that it discloses an entirely new historical phase; for we must be forced to the conclusion that the Lacedemonians were descendants of the Hamitic race. It would further lead us to infer that their rivals, the Athenians, were of Semitic descent. This is no rash conjecture, for we learn from the inscriptions that the Cushite Pharaoh Naifaurot had sent a fleet of one

Brugsch, vol. ii. 335.

hundred ships laden with corn, arms, and munitions of war, to the aid of the Lacedemonians; it is, therefore, apparent that this Pharaoh was independent of the Persian Elamites; hence the Cushite house of David (*i. e.* Hirhor) is again in possession of Egypt, and the dynasty, with considerable splendour, retain their power during a period of some sixty or seventy years, when they are again overthrown by the Persian Elamites under their great king Ochus. The Elamites are, however, hastening to their fall; and seven or eight years after Alexander, the great Macedonian warrior, defeats the Persian Elamites, and secures dominion over the entire empire; but, as I have shown, there were only two great races contending for supremacy, Alexander's conquest discloses that the Macedonians were also Cushites; and this is solidly confirmed when we find that Alexander showed his respect for the ancient religion by joining in the worship of Apis, and by going to the Oasis of Ammon to lay his offering as the "Son of the Sun" on the altar of Amen-Ra; we may be confident that he had some hereditary claim to the title.

I have pointed out that the Cushites were on the most friendly terms and in league with the Lacedemonians, who were in conflict with the Persian Elamites.

It is palpably obvious that historians have obscured the Greek Communities; we know that they were split up into two great factions, which is not accounted for; might we not reasonably conjecture that Greece was colonized by the Hamitic and Semitic races, and that the same contest for supremacy existed in Greece as in the Asiatic Empire. If this view is a correct one the Macedonians would represent the Cushite flag, and we are aware that they secured dominion by overthrowing the Persian Elamite power; but when we discover that history has been systematically distorted, may we not surmise that the Macedonian Cushites only held their power during the life-time of their Great King Alexander.

Undoubtedly a revolution did take place at his death, which historians have by no

See Juventus Mundi, W.E. Gladstone, chapter v. 118 2nd Edition.

means clearly explained; for we only gather that Greeks became dominant, which indicates no racial distinction. It follows, then, according to my reasoning, that these Greeks must have secured power under the Elamite flag. The Elamites would therefore be again dominant having subjugated the Cushites under the house of Alexander.

Following my argument; when we find that the Romans supplanted these Greeks, we must conclude that the Romans would have acquired dominion under the Cushite flag. This is strikingly confirmed; for we find that the Cushite Jews, who we must clearly understand represented the whole Cushite party in the empire, did enter into an alliance with the Romans. "So they went unto Rome, and entered into the Senate, and said, Jonathan the high priest and the people of the Jews sent us unto you, to the end ye should renew the friendship which ye had with them, and league as in former time." Under these circumstances we must view this record as a very remarkable confirmation of my argument.

We must therefore understand that the

I. Maccabees, xii. 3.

Cushites are again in power under the Roman flag, and the Elamites would be the opposition party.

Let us enquire whither the great Elamite party has vanished; we know they were in full power under their great King Cyrus and his dynasty. They had been deposed in Egypt by the Cushites under Amyrtæus of the house of David (*i.e.* Hirhor), but Ochus, of the Elamite house of Cyrus, recovered the empire; and Darius III. had fallen gallantly contending with Alexander. Although driven from power for some twenty years they again recovered dominion under the Greek flag, and held it during two hundred and eighty years. Surely, when the Romans under the Cushite flag superseded them, they must still have formed a strong opposition.

I must contend that I have conclusively proved that the characters represented in the Biblical narratives are genuine historical personages. That Chedorlaomer was the Great King of Elam who ruled from Elam to Thebes. That Abraham was a mighty chieftain of the Cushite race who supplanted him. That Moses was Apepi, the last of the so-called Hyksos Pharaohs, who was deposed by the Elamite Pharaoh Aahmes, the Joseph of the Old Testament. That Saul was the Elamite Pharaoh Ramses XII. That Esh-baal was the Elamite Pharaoh Ramses XIII. That David was the Cushite Pharaoh Hirhor who deposed him. That the Pharaoh Shishak was the son and vassal of Naromath the Great King of Elam. That Solomon, a junior branch of the Cushite house of David, reigned under the Elamite flag. That Isaiah was the Elamite Pharaoh Usargon. That Sabakah, the So of the Old Testament, was a Pharaoh of the senior house of David. That Nebuchadnezzar was Cyrus I., the Great King of Elam, and grandfather of Cyrus, the would-be Persian of the Old Testament. That Jeremiah was the Pharaoh Aahmes who supplanted the Cushite Pharaoh Apries. That Ishmael was the Pharaoh Psamethik who deposed Aahmes. That Daniel was the Cushite King Nabonidus. That Cyrus, the would-be Persian, was the Great King of Elam who supplanted Nabonidus and the Cushite Pharaoh Psamethik.

Philistines and Israelites.

Although I submit that each of these illustrious characters can readily be identified behind the sacerdotal masks, we must not take and judge the disguises only in detail. They are part of a general policy; they reflect light on each other; and taken together vividly expose the subtle wiles of priestcraft.

I now lift another veil which throws a flood of light on the world's history.

I am treading on very delicate ground, but truth must be followed at all hazards.

I have pointed out that all the great characters in the Biblical narratives are genuine historical personages; they have simply been masked to support the priestly design.

Abraham, Moses (*i.e.* Apepi), David (*i.e.* Hirhor) were great Cushite potentates; Isaiah and Jeremiah were Elamite Pharaohs; Cyrus was an Elamite Great King. They have, however, been presented to us in a sacerdotal garb. Instead of monarchs possessing vast worldly dominion, they are disclosed as of low origin and shorn of worldly prestige, but endowed with supernatural power as vice-gerents of the Eternal.

On the rise of the Cushite party under the Roman flag the great Elamite race seems to disappear. This could not have been the case; their power may have been bent but not broken, so let us endeavour to trace some indication of their presence. A great character certainly fills the horizon. Need I point to Jesus; and may we not view him as the representative of the great Elamite royal family? The name Jesus is equivalent to Hoshea, Joshua, and Joseph, royal Elamite family names.

See Smith's Dictionary of the Bible, Joshua.

The Cushite Jews and the Romans would see in him the central hope of the Elamite power. We gather from the records that Jesus claimed to be king; and if we read between the lines of the Gospel of Nicodemus, a revolution is clearly indicated. It is manifest that Jesus was acknowledged as King and God, by the Elamites, who are alluded to as Persians, Magi, and wise men from the East, which adroitly obscures the high political importance of their homage. It is also clearly recorded that Jesus ad-

See Gospel of Nicodemus. Suppressed Books of the original New Testament. S. Matthew xxvii. 37.

S. Matthew ii. 2.

vanced his claim to the throne through the Cushite line of David and Abraham. Thus, we can only conclude that the Greek and Roman dynasties did not represent the true ancient royal families. In this case we could understand that a large party of both races would be waiting, and are waiting, for their Messiah, or true King and God. Again my argument seems strangely confirmed; and if we could trace the rise of the Elamite party to Constantine, we might date the rise of Christendom and the Papal power to this period.

We are taught to believe that the early Biblical narratives were written by Moses, Joshua, and Samuel; if such is the case it proves that historical archives were kept in their minutest details. We know that the scribe's office from earliest times was a high and important one; and, from the monuments alone, students have been enabled to compile a consecutive history relating to political and social events. We can only conclude that the official records, written on imperishable clay tablets, were carefully preserved from time immemorial; and yet

S. Matthew, i. 1.

we are invited to believe that in the time of Homer no written records existed in Greece, and that his works, handed down by oral tradition, give us the only insight we could gain into early Grecian history. I assert with every confidence that Greece and Italy, as well as Egypt and Carthage, were dominated by the Hamitic and Semitic races. When, therefore, we view the Greeks as the descendants of the Cushite Pharaohs, and the Great Elamite Kings, the very stones cry out from their tombs to denounce the imposition.

We may assure ourselves that every available shred of historical evidence, inconsistent with the priestly design, has been garbled or obliterated.

I must contend that the Biblical records are incomprehensible unless we realise the two hostile races, and understand that they viewed their Great Kings as Gods. We dare not presume to imagine that the Eternal condescends to embroil himself in political struggles; yet every line in the priestly narratives seems to convey such an impression. We see, as it were in a transformation scene, the two great rival races and their two religious cults confounded together and insensibly blending into one race and one religion. Mark the consummate craft displayed in the combinations, which lead us to infer supernatural agency. I will instance two of very many similar records: "Jehoiachin was eight years old when he began to reign, and he reigned three months and ten days in Jerusalem: and he did that which was evil in the sight of the Lord. And when the year was expired, King Nebuchadnezzar sent, and brought him to Babylon." Surely it can only mean that Jehoiachin offended the Great King, and was deposed. Again, "Zedekiah was one and twenty years old when he began to reign, and he did that which was evil in the sight of the Lord his God, and humbled not himself before Jeremiah the prophet speaking from the mouth of the Lord, but stiffened his neck, and hardened his heart from turning unto the Lord God of Israel." The moment we recognise that Nebuchadnezzar was the Lord God of Israel—that is, the Great Elamite King—the narratives become consistent with common sense.

II. Chron. xxxvi. 9.

II. Chron. xxxvi. 11.

The insidious aim of the writers is palpably exposed; for upon these records is founded a claim of Divine right to imperial power and universal dominion.

CHAPTER XII.

THE HEBREWS.

I SUBMIT with every confidence I have conclusively proved that only the two powerful races of Shem and Ham were competing together for supremacy in the Eastern Empire; it is no conjecture, but a historical fact which cannot be questioned; for we have it unequivocally recorded that the races of Shem and Ham were paramount. If my view is not a tenable one, where can we trace these races?

Genesis x. 1.

Great confusion has resulted through historians not sufficiently emphasizing racial distinctions; for instance, the racial origin of the Normans is far from clearly defined, and they have become almost obliterated among the French and English.

Again, large sections of the Saxon race (probably Japhetic) are becoming lost to view under the territorial designations of

Americans, Canadians, and Australians; just as the Hamitic race has been concealed under the names of Hyksos, Philistines, and Ethiopians; and the Semitic race has been obscured under the names of Israelites, Assyrians, Chaldeans, and Persians.

Although the priestly writers inform us that the races of Shem and Ham were dominant, a third power is dimly placed on the scene; for we are led to infer from the Biblical narratives that the would-be Hebrew race of Jacob acquired supremacy under Joseph (*i.e.*, Aahmes), and retained their position for several generations, when they were subjugated by the Hamitic Pharaoh Khuenaten, and their forces were expelled from Egypt.

As we have only the two races before us let us distinctly understand to which of these races the Philistines and the Israelites belonged. Beyond a doubt the Israelites were represented by Joseph, the Semitic Pharaoh Aahmes; and as the so-called Hyksos represent the race of Father Ham (*i.e.*, Abraham), and the Philistines were a section of this race, it follows that the Philistines personated the Hamitic race; hence, when we find the Philistines and Israelites in conflict at Gilboa, this battle must represent a struggle for supremacy in the empire between the Hamitic and Semitic races.

It becomes then glaringly apparent that the priestly writers have designated them as Philistines and Israelites for the purpose of obscuring the two great races.

The Biblical writers allude to the pseudo-Saul as King of the Israelites; but Josephus refers to him as King of the Hebrews; we are therefore insidiously led to believe that the Israelites were Hebrews. I must contend that it is a glaring imposition, and one of the subtle combinations in the plot. The Israelites were a Semitic race and uncircumcised; the Philistines were of Hamitic descent and circumcised. This is practically confirmed, for the Hyksos Philistine Jews of the present day are circumcised.

We have been adroitly led to infer that the race of Jacob and Joseph was Hebrew; and as Jacob's name is ingeniously changed into Israel, the Hebrews and the Israelites appear as one race.

Philistines and Israelites.

We must carefully bear in mind, if we rely on the Biblical narratives, that the *Hebrews alone* are God's chosen people, and sole heirs to the Divine promises; it follows that the Biblical cult is centred in the Hebrews to the exclusion of any other race. If then the Hebrews were the only special objects of the Almighty's protection, it became vital to the priestly design that the two great races should be obscured and confounded into one. We can therefore detect the object the writers had in view when they insensibly lead us to infer that the Hamitic race of Abraham and the Semitic race of Jacob were both Hebrews.

Commentators are clearly at their wits' end to explain this, and are by no means agreed as to who the Hebrews were; and high ecclesiastical authorities go so far as to class them with Heber; but this clashes with the priestly historians, for it is recorded that Abraham himself was a Hebrew. This *Genesis xiv. 13.* probably was the case, but as it was vital to the priestly design that the two great Hamitic and Semitic races should be confused together, we are also informed that Joseph

Philistines and Israelites.

Genesis xxxix. 14.

was a Hebrew. He is not only a Hebrew, but Palestine, from whence he migrated, was in possession of the Hebrews. Moses also is represented as a Hebrew. We are therefore adroitly led to infer that the race of Abraham and the race of Jacob were Hebrews, and the two great rival races are thus subtlely confounded together, which insensibly leads us to infer that the Hebrews were in possession of their promised land. I must however contend that the house of Jacob or Joseph represents the Semitic race, and the house of Abraham or Moses points out the Hamitic race, and as these two races were constantly struggling together for supremacy in the empire, it was vital to the priestly plot, not only that the two great rival races should be obscured, but also the empire for which they were competing.

This has been ingeniously overcome by focussing our attention on the two small provinces of Judea and Israel, and by masking the two rival races under the name of Hebrews, which cleverly obliterates both the empire and the two rival powers. But as we find the Philistines and Israelites

Philistines and Israelites.

engaged in constant conflicts, they become conspicuously identified as the representatives of the two hostile races.

After the death of Moses the contest for supremacy continued during three or four centuries, when we have it recorded that a general engagement took place at Gilboa, where the Israelites (*i.e.* Elamites) suffered a crushing defeat, leaving the Philistines (*i.e.* Cushites) absolute masters of the country; and David becomes king over Western Asia. David then must have secured his empire under the Philistine (*i.e.* Cushite) flag. But when we find that at this moment a great revolution took place, and a dynasty falls, which had ruled from Elam to Thebes for nine generations, it follows that David must have overthrown this dynasty.

The inscriptions absolutely confirm this; for we learn from them that a Pharaoh, who bore the name of Hirhor, overthrew the Ramessides and became supreme from the Euphrates to Ethiopia. The reader will notice that this covers David's dominion, which indicates that David and Hirhor must have been identical monarchs.

I. Samuel xxxi. 7.

II. Samuel viii. 3.

Philistines and Israelites.

The inscriptions again confirm this, for Hirhor, who was a high priest of Amen and Prince of Cush, also bore the name of Nsbindidi, which is an equivalent to David, as I have already explained.

It therefore becomes manifest that the Philistines and Israelites of the Biblical narratives must represent the two rival flags of Cush and Elam.

It must strike us as remarkable that when we have a book purporting to be a history of the Hebrews, no one is able to define their origin or localise them. They certainly haunt the narratives like phantoms, but are never disclosed in any commanding position; they are introduced to us as slaves, are found occupying subordinate offices whenever alluded to, and at the fall of Jerusalem are discovered in servitude.

Jeremiah xxxiv. 9.

We seem to be lost in a sea of confusion, and naturally refer to the Bible dictionary which may be regarded as the concentrated essence of sacerdotal sophistry.

Smith's Dictionary of the Bible.

We turn first to "Hebrews" only to find a record of assumptions "utterly at variance" with each other; and we close the book bewildered in a cloud of "grossly improbable" conjectures.

We then turn to "Philistines" and find them also wrapped up in impenetrable mystery. Amid these conflicting efforts to explain away the palpable meaning of the term Hebrews, which would certainly apply to those who "crossed over"; might we not reasonably conjecture that the Cushites under Abraham acquired the name of Hebrews owing to their conquering hosts having "crossed over" from the far east when they subjugated the Elamites (*i.e.* Israelites) in Egypt and Western Asia.

Let us now endeavour to fathom the part the Hebrews are allotted to play in the priestly drama.

I have pointed out that only two great races existed within the Eastern empire, ever struggling for supremacy.

It was clearly vital to the priestly design that these two races should not only be obscured, but blended into one.

Hence, when we find Abraham the Cushite and Joseph the Elamite alluded to as Hebrews, cannot we detect that the Hebrews

Genesis xiv. 13; xxxix. 14.

Philistines and Israelites.

serve as the link which binds the two rival races together.

As we know that the so-called Hyksos had ruled over Egypt and probably Western Asia during a period of seven hundred years, certainly a rival race must have supplanted them; and the priestly writers (who, Cardinal Newman tells us, controlled all historical archives) have adroitly concealed them.

The Hebrews, then, subtlely masked to represent both rival races, are placed on the scene as God's chosen people and sole heirs of the Divine promises. It is precisely the combination needed to carry out the priestly design, for it insensibly blends the two great races together, and we are led to believe that the kings of Judea and Israel represented a common Hebrew monarchy; hence the Hebrews appear as possessors of their promised land.

But when the inscriptions inform us that only two great races were struggling for supremacy in the empire, it follows that one or the other of these races must be supreme. This is absolutely confirmed by the in-

Philistines and Israelites.

scriptions; for we find that the empire is governed alternately by the Elamites and the Cushites, as I have illustrated in my fourth chapter.

It becomes obvious that when the Elamites were in power the petty kings of Judea and Israel as well as the kings of all the provinces within the empire would be serving under the Elamite flag; and when the Cushites were supreme, the various petty kings would serve under the banner of Cush; consequently in times of peace and settled government, the two kings of Judea and Israel would beyond a doubt be flying the same flag as vassals of their great king; and as the fortresses were garrisoned by the forces of the Great King, it is impossible, under such circumstances, that the two kings could have been at war with each other; this could only have happened in times of revolution. We may, therefore, be absolutely certain when the king of Israel was at war with the king of Judea, that the Elamite flag flew over Samaria, and the Cushite flag flew over Jerusalem.

It is manifest, then, that the view of a

continuous Hebrew monarchy in Palestine is a delusion. The wars between the kings of Judea and Israel could only disclose a war between the Great King of Elam and the Great King of Cush : that is, a struggle for supremacy between the Semitic and Hamitic races.

I assert that the Hebrews, as an isolated dominant power, cannot be localized ; and I challenge students to identify them, unless they are recognised as the Hamitic race of Abraham, in which case the present Jews will represent the inheritors of the supposed Divine promises to the exclusion of the Israelites, or any other race.

Will the reader be good enough to pause for reflection ?

The Tel-el-Amarna tablets have disclosed that the Pharaohs of Egypt were viewed by their subjects as gods.

Khuenaten, the Cushite Pharaoh, who deposed the Elamite Pharaoh Amenhotep III., is styled by his officials as a deity: "To the king my Lord, my God, my Sun-God who is from Heaven," and as I assert that this Khuenaten was the Pharaoh

Philistines and Israelites.

"which knew not Joseph," it follows that Amenhotep, whom he deposed, was the Pharaoh who led the Israelites (*i. e.* Elamites) out of Egypt, which discloses a second Exodus. When, therefore, we read that "God led them not through the way of the land of the Philistines," we must understand that God here does not refer to the Almighty, but to the Pharaoh Amenhotep.

Exodus xiii. 17.

It becomes obvious that the record in question is a literal translation from the contemporary Egyptian archives, where all the Pharaohs are designated as gods. This will apply generally to all the Biblical records of a similar character, and must open our eyes to the subtlety of the priestly combinations.

It was vital to the priestly design that we should understand that the Hebrews were a special and God-protected race; and in some passages we are led to infer that they were a community distinct from the Israelites. But still the Biblical writers refer to Saul as the King of the Israelites, and Josephus alludes to him as the King of the Hebrews, leaving us to conjecture that the Hebrews and

I. Samuel xiv. 21.

Josephus, vol. i. 271.

the Israelites were one and the same people.

I must however contend that the Cushites of the Hamitic race represent the Hebrews, and the Elamites of the Semitic race represent the Israelites.

Apepi (*i.e.* Moses) led the Cushite Hebrews out of Egypt when overthrown by Aahmes (*i.e.* Joseph); and Amenhotep III. led the Elamite Israelites out of Egypt when defeated by Khuenaten.

These two distinct Exoduses have been designedly confounded into one, in order to obscure and blend together the two great hostile races.

At the battle of Gilboa the pseudo-Saul represents the Elamite Pharaoh Ramses XII. the so-called King of the Israelites; Achish the Philistine king of Gath represented the head of the house of Cush, the king of the so-called Hebrews. We may be morally certain that the Hamitic race was in conflict with the Semitic race. It follows that the so-called Hebrews (Cushites) and the so-called Israelites (Elamites) were two distinct peoples, hostile in race and religion.

Philistines and Israelites.

The priestly writers had not only to blend together the two races, but also to confound the two religions.

This transformation scene has been very ingeniously contrived; the two great rival races are first obscured under the names of Philistines and Israelites, and then presented to us as Hebrews, practising a common religion.

It was claimed that Jesus was the lineal descendant and head of both the Hamitic and Semitic ancient royal families; and as he was regarded as a Deity, the two religions would become amalgamated.

The Hamitic Jews, however, refused to acknowledge him; and hence the two hostile cults at present existing.

Gospel of Nicodemus, ii. 7.

CHAPTER XIII.

LAWS AND RELIGION.

LET us now glance at the legal and religious aspect.

There may have been many religious sects within the vast Eastern Empire; but, as I have shown that only two great races exercised supreme power, we may assure ourselves that the two religious cults, as defined in the inscriptions, were generally adopted throughout the length and breadth of the land.

We find, however, that both these cults are adroitly concealed by the priestly writers; but still we detect that after revolutions had taken place, religious reforms ensue in the small provinces of Judea and Israel.

For instance, when Sabakah of the Cushite house of David (*i.e.* Hirhor) overthrew the Assyrian Elamite government, and Hezekiah rebelled against the King of Assyria

*II. Kings xviii. 7.
II. Chron. xxix.*

Philistines and Israelites.

"and served him not," a complete religious revolution is recorded ; and, as such reforms may be detected after every change of government, we are forced to the conclusion that the two races followed two different cults.

Let us now endeavour to trace whether the worship conducted in the temple in Jerusalem was consistent with the creed as indicated in the priestly version of the books of Moses. We may reasonably conjecture that Moses (*i.e.* Apepi) did draw up a code of laws for his people ; but we may be confident that it was based on the old Cushite cult, and had but little sympathy with Elamite worship.

We have solid grounds for believing that Josiah of the house of Solomon, a junior branch of the house of David, secured his position on the throne of Judea under the Elamite flag. As the two royal families were united in blood relationship, Josiah was half Cushite and half Elamite ; so there is nothing to surprise us in finding the junior members of David's house in opposition to the elder branch. David himself had served under Ramses XII.; his son Absolom had adopted the Elamite flag, and Solomon had accepted office under Shishak, the Assyrian Elamite Pharaoh. Josiah, therefore, had only followed his family policy.

II. Kings xxiii. 29.

There cannot be a doubt of this, for the Pharaoh Necho of the senior branch of the house of David (*i.e.* Hirhor) is recorded to have invaded his country and slain Josiah at Megiddo. It therefore becomes manifest that Josiah was flying the Elamite flag, and the reforms he is recorded to have instituted indicated the suppression of the Cushite worship. If, then, we follow the reforms, we should, if we could rely upon them, ascertain the Cushite religious formula.

II. Kings xxii.

"Josiah was eight years old when he began to reign, and he did that which was right in the sight of the Lord. And Hilkiah the high priest said unto Shaphan the scribe, I have found the book of the law in the house of the Lord. And it came to pass when the King had heard the words of the book of the law, that he rent his clothes. And the King commanded Hilkiah the priest, Go ye, inquire of the Lord for me, and for the people and for all Judah, concerning the words of this book that is found: for great is the wrath of the Lord that is kindled against us, because our fathers have not hearkened unto the words of this book. And the King commanded Hilkiah the high priest to bring forth out of the temple of the Lord all the vessels that were made for Baal, and for the grove, and for all the host of heaven. And he put down the idolatrous priests, whom the Kings of Judah had ordained to burn incense in the high places. Them also that burned incense unto Baal, to the sun, and to the moon, and to the planets, and to all the hosts of heaven. And he brought out the grove from the house of the Lord, without Jerusalem, unto the brook Kidron, and burnt it there; and he brought all the priests out of the cities of Judah, and defiled the high places. And he defiled Topheth, that no man might make his son or his daughter to pass through the fire to Molech. And he took away the horses that the Kings of Judah had given to the sun, and burned the chariots of the sun with fire. And the altars which the Kings of Judah had made, and which Manasseh had made, and the high places that were before Jerusalem, which were on the right hand of the mount of corruption, which Solomon had builded for Ashtoreth the abomination of the Zidonians, and for Chemosh the abomination of the Moabites, and for Milcom the abomination of the children of Ammon, did the King defile; and he slew all the priests of the high places that were there on the altars, and burned men's bones upon them, and returned to Jerusalem. And the King commanded all the people, saying, Keep the passover. Surely there was not holden such a passover from the days of the judges that judged Israel, nor in all the days of the Kings of Israel, nor of the Kings of Judah."

The Abydus tablet informs us that soon after the death of David, the Assyrians, who represent the Elamite power, overthrew David's dynasty, and expelled the Cushite forces to Ethiopia. Shishak (*i.e.* Sargon) the son of the Great King, was placed on the throne of Egypt, and his family remained in power for some two hundred

See also Joseph Jacobs' articles on the Nethinim in the Babylonian and Oriental Record, vol. ii. pp. 66 and 100.

Brugsch, vol. ii. 211.

Ibid. 234.

years as vassals to the Great Elamite King who governed the entire empire from Nineveh to Thebes.

We learn that the house of David, under the Pharaoh Sabakah advancing from Ethiopia, reconquered Egypt from the Assyrians; and Hezekiah of the house of Solomon, allying himself with Sabakah, threw off his allegiance to the Great Assyrian King; we can, therefore, only conclude that Hezekiah continued his reign over Jerusalem under the flag of Cush; but clearly the Assyrian Elamite flag was flying over Jerusalem at the time of Josiah, or the Pharaoh Necho would not have attacked him at the close of his reign.

We have it recorded that Josiah did that which was right in the sight of the Lord, but that the wrath of the Lord was greatly kindled against him owing to the religious rites practised in Jerusalem, which were manifestly Cushite; and we are informed that Josiah sent Hilkiah to inquire of the Lord for him.

Beyond a shadow of doubt the Lord here simply refers to the great king.

The reader must bear in mind that the great kings were recognised as deities; the inscriptions solidly prove this as I have already pointed out. Can there be a doubt, then, that Josiah was appealing to his King and God.

We can only conclude that the Great King ordered Josiah to suppress the Cushite worship of the house of David; and, as we are aware that Assur was the great God of the Assyrians, we may be certain that the worship of Assur replaced the Cushite cult.

Again, when we know that David (*i.e.* Hirhor) was the high priest of Amen, we may assure ourselves that the worship of Assur replaced the worship of Amen. It becomes, then, very significant when we find that neither of these great Gods are mentioned by the priestly writers in connection with Josiah's reforms.

II. Kings xviii. 22.

We are informed that the suppression of the Cushite ritual by Josiah led to the celebration of the Passover amid general rejoicings. We are led to enquire what religious festival this passover commemorated. I submit that there can be no doubt as to

Philistines and Israelites.

this. It recalled the retreat of the Cushite Jews from Egypt under Moses (*i.e.* Apepi). It would therefore be the one festival that the great Elamite King would have interdicted.

The object of the priestly writers for inserting the record is obvious, for it subtly obscures the two great races and leads us to infer that they had a common worship and a common origin.

If we could rely on the records the reforms would disclose the Cushite ritual; but we may be sure that they are adroitly distorted to obscure the two paramount religions; but if they are authentic it certainly proves that the rites practised within the temple of Jerusalem were not in accordance with the ritual as indicated in the priestly version of the books of Moses.

Where was the niche in this temple for the two stone tablets said to have been written by the finger of the Almighty?

"Thou shalt have no other gods before me. Thou shalt not make unto thee any graven image, or any likeness of anything that is in heaven above, or that is in the earth beneath, or that is in the water under the earth. Thou shalt not bow down thyself to them, nor serve them."

It, therefore, becomes clear that such a creed was not preached in the Temple of Jerusalem.

If my assertion is correct, and Moses, the great lawgiver, represents the Pharaoh Apepi who led the Cushites into Judea where they became known as Jews; then we should find the code of laws in force among the Cushite Jews identical with the Egyptian code.

Professor Huxley, Evolution of Theology.

Professor Huxley points out that the Biblical ten commandments are almost identical with the Egyptian ten words, and follow each other in a similar rotation.

We can only conclude that the missing ones have been distorted by the priestly writers, in order to frame upon them an entirely different cult.

EGYPTIAN.	JEWISH.
3rd. I have not blasphemed.	3rd. Thou shall not take the name of the Lord thy God in vain.

Philistines and Israelites. 215

EGYPTIAN.	JEWISH.
5th. I have not reviled my Father.	5th. Honour thy Father.
6th. I have not murdered.	6th. Thou shalt do no murder.
7th. I have not committed adultery.	7th. Thou shalt not commit adultery.
8th. I have not stolen.	8th. Thou shall not steal.
9th. I have not told falsehood in the tribunal of truth.	9th. Thou shalt not bear false witness.

Hence it becomes apparent that the Jewish laws were not promulgated on Mount Sinai, but were derived from their ancient Cushite Egyptian code; and it solidly confirms my assertion that Apepi (*i.e.* Moses), a follower of the Sun God, Masu, instituted them.

We may further conclude that the worship and laws of the Elamites were framed upon an entirely different system. The two races could not have had a common house of worship; and we may be morally certain that the Elamite Israelities were in no way associated with any Jewish temple or passover. *II. Samuel vi. 7.*

At a much later date we have it recorded that the Jews had no dealings with the *S. John iv. 9.*

Philistines and Israelites.

Samaritans; in these Samaritans we can recognise the Elamites, subtly obscured under another name.

When we learn from the inscriptions—that the Gods, Assur, Nebo, Bel, and Merodach, were worshipped in Asia, and the great Egyptian cult was followed in Egypt, it becomes very remarkable that these great religious systems should be viewed by the people of Palestine as false and idolatrous.

But when Moses, Khuenaten, and David are disclosed as high priests of Amen, that is of the Sun God Masu or Aten, and we learn that David founded the temple in Jerusalem, it becomes absolutely certain that this temple was dedicated to the Sun God Amen. This is solidly confirmed when we find that the altar was decorated with rams-horns, the undoubted symbol of Amen-Ra.

An inscription, only lately discovered, informs us that the worship of Osiris, Horus, Isis, and Bast, did flourish in Palestine down to the third century B.C.; we may therefore be morally certain that

Egyptian Exploration Fund, April, 1892.

there were only two great religions and two great races exercising paramount influence within the empire.

When the Elamites were in power the Elamite cult was the state religion; when the Cushites were supreme their worship was dominant.

The inscriptions very clearly point out that the two cults had a common basis, for we find that the Gods Apis and Amen are worshipped by both races. Herodotus tells us that a temple of Jupiter-Amen existed in Babylon in his day, and that almost all the gods worshipped in Greece came from Egypt. It certainly indicates that Greece was colonised by the two Hamitic and Semitic races. This would also apply to Italy, for we learn from Josephus that the worship of Isis was practised in Rome; consequently when the Greeks and Romans dominated the Eastern Empire no national change of religion is perceptible. Of necessity this view has been obscured by the priestly writers; but we may reasonably conjecture that the Christian religion is only a modern development of the Semitic worship, and that the present

Herodotus, 1, 181.

Josephus, Book xviii. ch. iii.

Roman Pontiff represents the head of the house of Elam.

S. Laing, Human Origins, 112.

Mr. Laing, in his interesting treatise on "Human Origins," concludes that the Egyptians were the most religious people in the world; and yet they are pointed out by the priestly writers as a race under the ban of the Almighty. Such a charge is always fulminated when one system of priestcraft clashes with another.

"There is but one God, and Mahomet is his Prophet," is the war cry of Islamism; and every priestly cult adopts a similar one. The supposed mediator between God and man is alone changed.

In this all peoples are agreed: There is but one God, the great Architect of the Universe.

The worship of the supreme being then the basis of all religions, it matters little how the Eternal is symbolised, or under what name he is worshipped. The virtuous and reverent of every nation follow one religion and one moral code.

While the world has been wrangling over incomprehensible dogmas the priests have

Philistines and Israelites.

been laughing in their sleeves and quietly pocketing the "first fruits."

A record worthy of remembrance is preserved in an old manuscript on papyrus, dating back to the fourth milennium B.C.: "It does the heart good, and refreshes the mind to follow that ancient discourse which unfolds the deepest thoughts of the venerable prince in simple, childlike words. Its teaching is noble as to the true greatness of man, for it is penetrated by the gentle spirit of human purity."

Patah-hotep speaks thus: "And if thou hast become great, after thou hast been lowly, and if thou hast amassed riches after poverty, so that thou hast become because of this the first in thy city; and if the people know thee on account of thy wealth and thou art become a mighty lord, let not thy heart be lifted up because of thy riches, for the author of them is God. Despise not thy neighbour, who is as thou wast; but treat him as thy equal." Has modern priestcraft developed a purer doctrine?

The Rev. E. Garbett, M.A., "Select Preacher and Boyle Lecturer," in a sermon preached before the University of Oxford, November 16, 1862, writes as follows: "If the belief in the infallibility of the Scriptures be a falsehood, the Church founded upon it must be a living fraud . . . in all consistent reason we must accept the whole of the inspired autographs, or reject the whole as from beginning to end unauthoritative and worthless."

I must submit that the Rev. E. Garbett is sternly logical, for it follows, if the Biblical narratives are not inspired by the Almighty, they are forgeries.

The Times, April 22nd, 1892.

M. Renan is reported to have stated: "It is better to have some kind of faith than to believe in nothing at all. To me religion is the indispensable necessity which alone satisfies the craving for the ideal in human nature in all latitudes; and what religion could better satisfy ideal aspirations than does the Catholic, with its mystic poetry and imposing, well-balanced pomp of its ceremonials?"

Such a conception would apply to every religion, and recalls the trite old saying, "Where ignorance is bliss 'tis folly to be wise."

Philistines and Israelites.

The question however naturally arises, Can we derive benefit from delusions, and are we tamely to sanction a class fattening upon them? I will leave my readers to form their own conclusions.

We have it recorded that the priest Hilkiah found the book of the law which revealed the precepts of the Almighty. Is it not high time to search for another such volume? *II. Kings xxii. 8.*

It will not be discovered by priest or pope.

It will not be found in any ecclesiastical library.

It will be entitled Philosophy and Science.

Will students and scholars endeavour to find it?

CHAPTER XIV.

RECAPITULATION.

I will now endeavour to condense my argument into as few words as possible.

We will commence from the XIIth Egyptian dynasty. It represented the greatest power in the world from about 2400 B.C. to 2200 B.C., when we learn from the inscriptions that it was supplanted by a foreign race coming from the far east. This race is known to us as the Hyksos, and it continued to exercise sovereignty during a period of 700 years.

We have, then, two periods of settled government in view, viz., the XIIth dynasty reigning for 200 years, and the Hyksos reigning for 700 years; hence during 900 years there was only one change of government. Surely we should be able to identify such a mighty revolution!

Genesis xiv. We gather from the Biblical narratives

Philistines and Israelites.

that a great revolution did take place about this period, and we find it recorded that Abraham defeated Chedorlaomer, the King of Elam, and acquired dominion over Western Asia.

Students have recognised in this Chedorlaomer the Khudur-Lagamar of the inscriptions, who reigned, according to the most probable calculations, 2200 B.C.

Story of the Nations, Chaldea, Ragozin, 224.

This conquest of Abraham must then of necessity synchronise with the fall of the XIIth Egyptian dynasty.

The mighty revolution is, therefore, disclosed. As we learn that Elam was the eldest son of Shem, and Cush was the eldest son of father Ham (Abraham), we can only conclude, when Abraham overthrew the power of Elam, that the Cushites had subjugated the Elamites.

Genesis x.

It follows that the people designated as Hyksos, who came into power on the fall of the XIIth dynasty, were Cushites; and further, that the XIIth dynasty represented the Elamites.

We have then the two great Hamitic and Semitic races vividly before us.

It becomes obvious, if we wish to understand the political organisation of the Eastern Empire, we must keep these two great races steadily in view. As it matters little how we designate them, I have, for the sake of avoiding confusion, followed them as Cushites and Elamites.

We must, therefore, understand that the Cushites had overthrown the power of Elam about 2200 B.C., and continued supreme during a period of 700 years. This brings us to 1500 B.C., when we learn from inscriptions that another change of government took place. The Cushite Hyksos dynasty is supplanted by a Pharaoh of the name of Aahmes. We are led to inquire what race Aahmes represented; common sense would certainly point to the Elamites. This view is practically confirmed by the monuments, for we have at Abydus a list of the Pharaoh Seti's ancestors. He claims all the Pharaohs of the XIIth dynasty, passes over all the Hyksos Pharaohs, and then claims the Pharaoh Aahmes.

We may, therefore, be morally certain Aahmes was an Elamite, and that he had brought the Elamite race again into power. If we read between the lines we shall find this is confirmed by the Biblical records, for, although garbled and distorted, they are based upon authentic history.

Let us remember that the Cushites had exercised dominion for 700 years, and were supplanted by Aahmes, whose dynasty continued to reign for 200 years. So we have again only one possible revolution to identify, between 2200 B.C. and 1300 B.C., a period of 900 years.

When, therefore, we find it shadowed in the Biblical narratives that Joseph came into power in Egypt, we are led to surmise that Joseph represents Aahmes.

Let us for the moment presume that this was the case, and if possible ascertain if such a view is consistent with reliable history.

It has been ascertained from the inscriptions, that the Cushite or Hyksos Pharaoh, deposed by Aahmes, bore the name of Apepi, and his forces were expelled from Egypt about 1500 B.C.; Aahmes (*i.e.* Joseph) succeeded him, and his dynasty continued in power for 200 years, when another revolution is disclosed and a Pharaoh of the name of Khuenaten secures the throne. It was not only a political, but a religious revolution, for Khuenaten removed his seat of government from Thebes and built his royal palace at Tel-el-Amarna, where he established the worship of the Sun God Masu or Aten; he is succeeded by three members of his family, Ra-saa-ka-Khepru, Tut-ankh-amen, and Ai, all ardent followers of the Sun God.

Prof. Flinders Petrie.

This revolution has not been detected by Egyptologists, for Khuenaten and his dynasty have been included with the Pharaohs of the XVIIIth dynasty; they are, however, there designated as heretic kings.

Seti's list of ancestors, however, explains that Khuenaten and his three successors were not of Seti's family or race, for he passes over these four Pharaohs as foreign to his dynasty. We may reasonably conclude that Khuenaten and his three successors were Cushites of the house of Abraham and Apepi. We may also further conclude

Philistines and Israelites.

that Khuenaten followed the same worship as did his ancestor Apepi.

Apepi, then, must have been a worshipper of the Sun God Aten or Masu; this will explain how Apepi became designated as Masu or Moses.

This is so important that I must risk wearying the reader with repetition. I will, therefore, notice again that Apepi was the last Pharaoh of the XVIIth Cushite or Hyksos dynasty; it had ruled 700 years when it was supplanted by the Elamite Pharaoh Aahmes (*i.e.* Joseph), whose dynasty continued in power for 200 years, hence there was only one change of government between 2200 B.C. and 1300 B.C., a period of 900 years.

Let us endeavour to discover the date of this singular and momentous event.

It has been ascertained that the temple of Jerusalem was built for the Jews about 1017 B.C., 480 years after their retreat from Egypt under a leader named Moses, that is, 1497 B.C.

I. Kings vi. I.

It becomes evident that the retreat of the Cushites or Hyksos from Egypt under Apepi must be identical with the retreat of the Jews under Moses. Apepi then must represent Moses, and these Jews must represent the Cushites or Hyksos. We must therefore understand that Moses represents the Hyksos Pharaoh Apepi, and that Aahmes who deposed him must represent Joseph. Joseph then must have deposed Moses.

It will not be denied that Joseph, Hoshea, and Joshua are synonymous names, so when we learn that Hoshea or Joshua the son of Nun held a conference with Moses, and Moses was very soon after spirited away, we have it practically confirmed that Joseph (*i.e.* Joshua) did depose Moses.

Deuteronomy xxxii. 44; xxxiv.

Exodus i. 6.

We further learn from the records that "Joseph died, and all his brethren and all that generation, when there arose a new king which knew not Joseph."

Judges ii. 8.

We again find it recorded that "Joshua died, and also that generation, and there arose another generation after them which knew not the Lord." As the Lord here clearly refers to the Pharaoh, the two records are practically identical. We are therefore forced to the conclusion that

Joseph and Joshua are identical personages, and, as the inscriptions inform us, that a Pharaoh named Aahmes supplanted Apepi (*i.e.* Moses) it becomes manifest that Aahmes, Joshua, and Joseph are synonymous terms, and not distinct characters as represented in the Biblical narratives.

When we are informed that some time after the death of Aahmes (*i.e.* Joseph) a new king arose "which knew not Joseph," we can only infer that a change of government took place, and as I have pointed out that Khuenaten, a worshipper of the Sun God Masu or Aten, did bring the Cushites into power, we may be morally certain that Khuenaten was the Pharaoh "which knew not Joseph" (*i.e.* Aahmes); and we gather from the Biblical records he reduced the Israelites (*i.e.* the Elamites) to slavery and expelled them from Egypt, just as Aahmes (*i.e.* Joseph) had expelled the Cushites 200 years previously. Here then we have two exoduses from Egypt before us, and the priestly writers have adroitly confounded them together.

But still we may easily separate them, for

Philistines and Israelites.

we find that the Cushites under Apepi (*i.e.* Moses) were not reduced to slavery, but retreated in force to Judea, where they intrenched themselves in their strongholds on the sea coast, and became called Philistines, giving their name to the country they dominated as Philistia. That it had no connection with the exodus of the Elamite or Israelite slaves is apparent, for we learn that the slaves did not retreat to Judea, but followed the road to the east of the Dead Sea and entered the Province of Israel by crossing the Jordan at Jericho. Here we detect the second exodus. "And it came to pass when Pharaoh (*i.e.* Khuenaten) had let the people go, that God led them not through the way of the land of the Philistines, although that was near, for God said, lest peradventure the people repent when they see war, and they return to Egypt."

The reader will notice that the Pharaoh of Egypt is here alluded to, as it is in very many other instances, as Pharaoh; this is a palpable blunder, and craftily adopted to obscure the Pharaoh's name.

We must also remember that the Pharaohs

Exodus xiii. 7.

were recognised as Divine beings, and designated as Gods.

The record is undoubtedly authentic and extracted word for word from the Egyptian archives; and we may be morally certain that the deposed Elamite Pharaoh, Amenhotep III., led his forces from Egypt and retreated beyond the Euphrates; when, therefore, we read "that God led them not through the way of the land of the Philistines," it simply means that Amenhotep III. avoided the Cushite troops in their strongholds of Judea.

It is obvious that the Cushites under Khuenaten had expelled the Elamite forces from Egypt just as Aahmes (*i.e.* Joseph) had expelled the Cushites under Apepi (*i, e.* Moses).

The Philistines, then, in Judea would represent a section of the Cushites, and the Israelites of the tribe of Judah must represent a section of the Elamites. This is confirmed, for we find that the Philistines and the Israelites were hostile to each other and continually struggling for supremacy.

The Cushites under their Pharaoh Khue-

Philistines and Israelites.

naten were now in power in Egypt, and his dynasty continued supreme for some eighty years, when it was supplanted by the Elamites under their Pharaoh, Horemhib; this is confirmed, for we find that Seti claims him as one of his ancestors.

Horemhib is succeeded by Ramses I., Seti I., and Ramses II., and the inscriptions disclose that Ramses II. was engaged during all his long reign in defending his position against the attacks of the Cushites, when a treaty was concluded between the two rival races, which left them, as Dr. Brugsch tells us, the two greatest nations in the world.

Brugsch, vol ii. 76.

We have, therefore, the Cushites under their king Khita-sir ruling in Asia, and the Elamites under their Pharaoh, Ramses II., ruling in Egypt.

A royal marriage cemented this solemn treaty, and Ramses II. married the Cushite king's daughter. The two flags are, therefore, conspicuously before us.

This marriage united in blood relationship the two royal families; but, as we might have anticipated, it had but little influence in uniting the two rival races.

Philistines and Israelites.

Ramses II. was succeeded by Mineptah II., and constant struggles for supremacy are disclosed both in the Biblical narratives and the inscriptions.

We learn from the priestly writers, "In those days there was no king in Israel, but everyone did that which was right in his own eyes." This is confirmed by the inscriptions, which inform us: "The people of Egypt lived in banishment abroad. Of those who lived in the interior of the land none had any care for him. So passed away long years. Whatever any had gathered together that his companions robbed them of. Thus did they."

It becomes clear that the solemen treaty has been broken, and the two rival races are as hostile to each other as ever.

The Elamite Pharaoh, Ramses III., appears to have obtained supremacy; and, as we find among his prisoners after a protracted campaign, "The king of the miserable land of Kush, and the miserable king of the Khita," we may be certain that the Cushites had been subjugated; and as the Ramesside dynasty continued to reign from father to

Judges xvii. 6.

Brugsch, vol. ii. 143.

Brugsch, vol. ii. 158.

son for nine generations, we can only conclude that a settled government was instituted; and we find Ramses XIIth exercising sovereign power from Ecbatana to Thebes. The flag of Elam must have floated over every fortress within the empire during a period of at least 100 years.

Brugsch, vol. ii. 191.

Another revolution is now disclosed both in the inscriptions and the Biblical narratives.

Hirhor, the hereditary king's son of Cush, rebels against the Elamite Pharaoh, Ramses XIIth, and succeeds in securing his throne.

Ibid. 200.

This Hirhor was Grand Vizier to Ramses XIIth, High Priest of Amen, and king's son of Cush. We must therefore conclude that his father was alive, who would have represented the dethroned king of the great Cushite race. He would therefore have led the rebellion against the Elamite Pharaoh. He is glaringly disclosed in the priestly narratives; for we find it recorded that Achish, the Philistine [Cushite] King of Gath, did rebel and became master in Palestine.

Brugsch, vol. ii. 200.

I. Samuel xiii. 19.

Two strange characters however appear

Philistines and Israelites.

on the scene. Saul, a man of low origin, is represented as King of the Israelites: "And there was sore war against the Philistines all the days of Saul." David, a shepherd lad, marries Saul's daughter, and becomes general-in-chief of Saul's forces. Saul kills his thousands, and David his ten thousands; David deserts Saul and goes over to the Philistines; a great battle takes place at Gilboa, between the Philistines and the Israelites, and the Israelites are utterly routed. Saul is killed in the battle, and as we hear nothing more of the Philistine king, Achish, we must conclude that he shared a similar fate. David succeeds Achish as King of the Philistines (*i.e.*, Cushites), and Esh-baal succeeds his father, Saul, as King of the Israelites (*i.e.*, Elamites); and we find it recorded that there was long war between the house of David and the house of Saul. David murders Esh-baal, the King of the Israelites; the Israelites tender their submission, and David becomes monarch from the Euphrates to Egypt.

We must, therefore, suppose that the Israelites, under Saul the stable boy, and

I. Samuel xiv. 52.

I. Samuel xxxi. 7.

II. Samuel iii. 1.

Philistines and Israelites.

the Philistines under David the shepherd lad, have been fighting for the crown of the Pharaoh Ramses; and the great Pharaoh, who had ruled from Ecbatana to Thebes, never interfered or struck one blow for his vast empire.

As it is the aim of the priestly writers to obscure the two races and confound them together, we are adroitly led to imagine that David was an Israelite (*i.e.* Elamite); although it is recorded that there was long war between the house of David and the house of Saul, it is also recorded that there was sore war against the Philistines all the days of Saul.

Now, if we must view David as an Israelite, it will be noticed that if there was sore war between Saul and the Philistines, and long war between David and Saul, we must understand that the Israelites were engaged in civil war; and, if we accept that David was in conflict with the Philistines, we must suppose that the Philistines were fighting both sections of the Israelite forces. Hence Saul would be at war with David and the Philistines, and David would be at war with

II. Samuel iii. 1.

I. Samuel xiv. 52.

Philistines and Israelites.

Saul and the Philistines; and the Philistines would be in conflict with both Saul and David.

Such a three-cornered position being contrary to reason, I must contend that the records leading us to believe that David was a simple Israelite shepherd boy, and a scourge to the Philistines, are only inserted with a view of leading us to infer that he was no Philistine. David's genealogy is given us; and, as we find he was descended from Abraham and Moses and so back to Adam, we can hardly credit that he was the drudge of a large family tending sheep on the hill side; but if we eliminate these egregious distortions we come to more reliable history, when we find David a general in the Philistine camp, living with Achish King of Gath.

1. Samuel xxvii. 2.

As the inscriptions inform us that the Pharaoh Hirhor bore also the name of Nisbindidi or David, the flagrant imposition foisted upon us in the priestly records becomes exposed. Although their narratives are distorted they are undoubtedly based upon authentic history, for we find them confirmed by the inscriptions in all essential particulars.

We must, therefore, understand that the great battle of Gilboa, represented in the narratives as an engagement between the Philistines and the Israelites, was a conflict between the Cushites and the Elamites which ultimately placed David (*i.e.* Hirhor) on the throne as the Pharaoh of Egypt.

1. Samuel xxxi. 7.

Dates are somewhat uncertain; but when we learn from the inscriptions that the Ramessides were in power for at least one hundred years, and were then deposed by Hirhor, whose dynasty ruled at least fifty years, only one change of government could have taken place within a period of one hundred and fifty years.

As all historians have accepted the Biblical records as divinely inspired and absolutely authentic, when it was ascertained that David's accession to power over Western Asia must have occurred about 1060 B.C., another date was of necessity adopted for the accession of Hirhor as the Pharaoh of Egypt and Western Asia.

Assyrian Eponym, Geo. Smith.

Brugsch, vol. ii. 202.

Hence we find a divergence of opinion;

but they are all agreed within a period of thirty-five years from 1035 B.C. for the rise of Hirhor to power.

Now, let us understand, we are endeavouring to fix the date of one possible revolution which occurred on the fall of the Ramessides who had ruled over Western Asia for at least one hundred years; and as the inscriptions disclose that Hirhor, an hereditary king's son of Cush, supplanted them, and his dynasty ruled for at least fifty years, how can the Biblical David's reign of forty years be possibly inserted?

But when the inscriptions inform us that Hirhor bore also the name of Nisbindidi, or David, it becomes absolutely certain that Hirhor represents David.

Maspero, Records of the Past, N. S. vol. v. 20.

The Cushites under David (*i.e.* Hirhor) were now supreme from the Euphrates to Ethiopia, and the Elamite forces would certainly have retired to their dominions on the east of the Euphrates.

David's dynasty had but a short rule; the Elamites, shortly after David's death, invaded the country from Assyria, and eventually Shishak, the son of the great Elamite

Assyrian King, was placed on the throne of Egypt. The Elamite flag must have again floated over every fortress in the Empire, and the Cushite forces must have retired to their dominions in Ethiopia.

Although many struggles for supremacy are recorded between the two rival races none were successful for a period of more than two hundred years, when the inscriptions disclose that Bokenranef, of the house of Hirhor (*i.e.* David) from Ethiopia, managed to reconquer Egypt and depose the Elamite Pharaoh Usarkon. Bokenranef succeeded in maintaining his seat on the throne, and is succeeded by Sabakah of the same house, who carried his arms into Western Asia.

II. Kings xvii. 4; xviii. 7.

Hoshea, the petty Elamite King of Israel, and Hezekiah, the petty king of Judea, throw off their allegiance to their Great King of Assyria; hence the Cushite flag would now wave over all the fortresses from Samaria to Ethiopia.

This brings Shalmaneser, the Great Elamite King, on the scene. Samaria after a long siege is taken, and Hezekiah is forced to hoist the Elamite flag over Jerusalem, and pay tribute to the Great King. The Cushite forces retiring to their fortresses on the sea coast and Egypt. A long series of engagements take place, and Jerusalem and Samaria are taken and retaken many times during the following fifty years, when Esarhadon succeeds in subjugating the Cushite Pharaoh Tirhakah and drives him back to his dominion in Ethiopia.

Tirhakah, however reconquers Egypt and is again expelled by Assurbanipal. The Cushites again rebel under Urdamaneh, but are again expelled.

Twenty kings or satraps are set up in Egypt as vassals to the Great Elamite King. Psamethik of the house of Cush secures ascendancy and assumes the double crown of Egypt; and, as we find his successor Pharaoh Necho warring against the Elamite Assyrians at Carchemish, which guarded the northern fords of the Euphrates, we may be absolutely certain that the Cushite flag, at this date, floated on every fortress from Carchemish to Ethiopia; and as we find that Nabopolassar the great king of Elam takes Nineveh, we may be equally certain that the Pharaoh Necho not only held Carchemish but Nineveh also; for who could possibly have taken and defended Nineveh against Nabopolassar, but the Cushites.

Nebuchadnezzar now becomes the Great King of Elam. The Pharaoh Necho was succeeded by Psamethik II. and Uahabra (the Hophra of the Bible, and the Apries of other historians).

Nebuchadnezzar takes Carchemish and invades Western Asia; he then besieges Jerusalem, hauls down the Cushite flag, and places Jehoiakin on the throne of Judea as his vassal; and, probably, a peace is concluded with Apries the Cushite Pharaoh of Egypt; but shortly after the Cushites again secure possession of Jerusalem; they are, however, expelled by the Great King, and Zedekiah is placed on the throne of Judea under the Elamite flag.

II. Chron. xxxvi. 13. Zedekiah continues to reign during eleven years under the Elamite flag, when he rebels against the Great King and hoists the Cushite flag. Nebuchadnezzar again invades

Philistines and Israelites.

the country, recaptures Jerusalem, and eventually carries his arms into Egypt, deposes the Cushite Pharaoh Apries, and places Jeremiah on the throne of Egypt known in the inscriptions as Aahmes, a name which recalls the Elamite Pharaoh Aahmes of the XVIIIth dynasty.

Josephus, vol. i. 428.

Every fortress within the Empire would now be garrisoned by Elamite troops, with the exception of the strongholds on the sea coast, which were protected by their war ships.

A peace was probably concluded, and the Cushite troops in Egypt retired to their dominion in Ethiopia.

Another rebellion is disclosed; the Elamites under their Great King Nebuchadnezzar again invade Western Asia and Tyre is besieged.

Ishamel leads his Philistine forces against the Elamite garrison in Mispath, and the Elamite troops are forced to retreat into Egypt; and, as the inscriptions inform us, that the Cushite Pharaoh Psamethik III. secured the throne of Egypt, we can only conclude that he deposed the Elamite

Pharaoh Aahmes (*i.e.* Jeremiah), and the forces of Nebuchadnezzar have been utterly routed.

We might well anticipate the fall of the Elamite power in the empire. This is solidly confirmed; for, as I have conclusively proved that there were only two great races struggling for supremacy, Nabonidus must have wrested the throne of Babylon from the Elamites under the flag of Cush; of this there can be no doubt, for it appears from a cylinder of Nabonidus that Syria and Phœnicia continued faithful to Nabonidus until the very last year of his struggle with Cyrus the Great King of Elam. We have, then, the Cushite Pharaoh Psamethik on the throne of Egypt, and the Cushite King Nabonidus on the throne of Babylon. The Cushite flag must have floated over every fortress from Babylon to Ethiopia. It becomes obvious that there could not have been any Cushite prisoners in the Eastern Empire at this period; for all the prisoners, taken by Nebuchadnezzar, on the fall of Jerusalem, would have been liberated.

The Story of the Nations, Rawlinson, Phœnicia, 185.

Philistines and Israelites.

The reader must notice that the priestly writers invite us to believe that the Elamite Great King Nebuchadnezzar took a vast number of Israelites into captivity on the fall of Jerusalem. It is, however, palpably apparent that Nebuchadnezzar's captives were the Cushite Philistine Jews; the Elamite Jews had naturally flocked into Judea on the rise of the Elamite power. It follows, that when the Cushite Nabonidus supplanted the dynasty of Nebuchadnezzar he would release all the Cushite prisoners taken by Nebuchadnezzar; hence, if any Elamite (*i.e.* Israelite) captives were prisoners in Babylon during the reign of Nabonidus, they must have been prisoners taken by Nabonidus; and when Cyrus, the Elamite King, deposed the Cushite Nabonibus, he would certainly release all the Elamite captives, and probably replace them with the Cushite prisoners he had himself taken captive during his victorious campaign. These prisoners have been so confounded together by the priestly writers, we are utterly bewildered; but let us remember that they are designedly confused for the

Ezra ii.

purpose of confounding the two great rival races. If we allow our reason scope, it is easily explained.

Nebuchadnezzar was the Great King of Elam, and his prisoners were Cushites. Nabonidus was a Cushite King, and his captives were Elamites. Cyrus was the Great King of Elam, and his prisoners were Cushites. It stands to reason, then, that the Jews taken prisoners by Nebuchadnezzar were Cushite Jews, and the Jews taken prisoners by Nabonidus were Elamite Jews. Again. The Israelites, that is the people residing in the province of Israel, taken captive by the Cushite Nabonidus were Elamite Israelites, and the Israelites taken captive by Cyrus were Cushite Israelites.

See I. Esdras.

The drama has been designed with consummate skill and is certainly very perplexing. The plot, however, becomes exposed the moment we recognise that the Hamitic and Semitic races permeated every province of the Empire, just as the Tories and Radicals permeate every county of Great Britain. The priestly writers, in order to obscure the two great rival races, have cunningly

Philistines and Israelites.

blended them together, and hence the confusion. Let me add, that priestcraft still carries on the deception; Christianity has confounded the races which are now as eagerly struggling for supremacy as ever. If students are clever enough to define the three races of Shem, Ham, and Japheth, the political situation of the present contests under home rule flags will be better understood.

Another great revolution is disclosed, and the priestly writers adroitly lead us to suppose that a foreign race appears upon the scene; with barefaced effrontery we are told that Cyrus a Persian defeats Nabonidus, and acquires dominion for the Persians over all Asia. The imposition is however exposed, for we learn from a cylinder of Cyrus, only lately discovered, that Cyrus was the Great King of Elam, and the descendant of a long and illustrious line of Elamite Kings.

During Cyrus' campaign he must have taken many captives; and, when he had consolidated his Asiatic Empire, a peace was naturally concluded, and his prisoners released. As we find it recorded that Zerubbabel, a prince of the Cushite house of David, leads these captives back to their homes from Babylon, it becomes glaringly evident that they were Cushites of the seed of Abraham, and not Israelites (*i.e.* Elamites).

Cyrus shortly after deposes the Cushite Pharaoh Psamethik, and places his son Cambyses on the throne as his vassal.

The Elamite flag must again have floated over every fortress from Elam to Thebes. The Philistine Cushites or Jews in their strongholds on the sea cost would become tributaries to the Great Elamite king, and the Cushite Egyptian forces would retire to their dominion in Ethiopia, where it is known that Cambyses followed them, and sustained a severe defeat; hence, we may conclude, that their power was by no means exhausted.

Herodotus, iii. 25.

The Elamite dynasty of Cyrus continued in power over the entire Asiatic Empire from about 527 B.C. to 332 B.C., a period of 195 years. But the Cushites, under their Pharaoh Amyrtæus, of the house of David, in league with their kindred the Spartans, wrested the dominion of Egypt from the Elamites in 424 B.C., and held it till 340, when the Elamites, under their Great King Ochus, again subjugated the country, and thus again became master of the entire empire from Elam to Thebes.

1. Maccabees xii. 21.

Another revolution is now disclosed. Alexander, designated by priestly historians as a Macedonian, invades Asia and secures dominion from the Indus to Ethiopia ; but, as I have proved, there were only two races struggling for supremacy ; and we have been so often imposed upon by territorial appellations, we may more than conjecture that Alexander acquired his empire under the Cushite flag. This is practically confirmed, for we find he adopts the old Cushite title of "Son of the Sun ;" and, we may reasonably infer, he could not have done so had he not some hereditary claim to the title. We must therefore understand that Alexander acquired dominion over the empire under the flag of Cush.

We have now followed the ups and downs of the Cushite and Elamite flags since the defeat of the Elamites under Chedorlaomer by the Cushites under Abraham, a period of some nineteen hundred years; and as we have found no foreign race intruding with the exception of the Scythians, who were probably a section of the Japhitic race, we may be morally certain that the Cushite flag of Alexander could only have been deposed to make way for the Elamite flag.

The priestly historians inform us that the Greeks came into power. It is palpably a designation which gives no indication of their race. We may therefore rest assured that it is only the old well-worn combination in the plot for the purpose of obscuring the Elamites. They have been imposed upon us as Hebrews, as Israelites, as Mesopotamians, as Syrians, as Egyptians, as Assyrians, as Jews, as Chaldeans, as Persians, as Samaritans, and now they appear as Greeks.

These Elamite Greeks retain their dominion over the empire for 275 years, when they are deposed by the Romans.

The Cushites have been masked as Hebrews, as Israelites, as Hyksos, as Philistines, as Cherithites, as Jews, as Babylonians, as Maccabees, as people of the land, as persons, and now they appear as Romans. From this we may reasonably conjecture that the Romans acquired dominion over the Eastern Empire under the flag of Cush. This remarkable phase, which must revolutionise our present conception of history, is practically confirmed, for we find it recorded that the Cushite Jews send an embassy to Rome. "So they went unto Rome and entered into the Senate and said: Jonathan the high priest, and the people of the Jews, send us unto you, to the end ye should renew the friendship which ye had with them, and league as in former times." *1. Maccabees xii. 3.*

The embassy also goes to Sparta, and we find it recorded: "It is found in writing that the Lacedemonians and Jews are brethren, and that they are of the stock of Abraham." *Ibid. xxi.*

It becomes evident, then, that the Cushites were leagued with the Romans and Spartans against the Elamite Greeks; hence the Cushite flag was paramount in the Empire.

When we view the political situation in this light a mighty revolution is disclosed. The great Elamite flag, which had floated over every fortress within the empire for nearly three hundred years, is now deposed, and the Elamite party retire into the cold shade of opposition.

We have now traced the alternate rise and fall of the Hamitic and Semitic races for 2400 years, and approach the closing scene in the priestly drama.

If we read between the lines of the Gospel of Nicodemus we may be absolutely certain that the Elamites rebelled against the Cushite rule, under Jesus, the head of the royal house of Elam. The name Jesus is an equivalent to Hoshea and Joshua, royal Elamite family names. He was undoubtedly hailed by the people as their king, and they address him under precisely the same title as we find the Great King is addressed in the Tel-el-Amarna tablets, "Lord who is from heaven," and as we are aware that the Great Kings were worshipped as deities, one of his titles would be "Son of God."

Dictionary of the Bible, Joshua.

Nicodemus, i. 12.

Palestine Exploration, October, 1892.

Philistines and Israelites.

I must submit that this unquestionably identifies Jesus as the head of the house of Elam. If further proof is needed we have only to turn to the record of his genealogy. It will be noticed he claims his descent through Solomon, the junior branch of the Cushite house of David; we shall remember that this family adopted the Elamite flag. His true royal descent would obviously be traced through the kings of the Elamite dynasties I have illustrated in Chapter IV., and Seti's list of ancestors. The reader will bear in mind that the Elamites were not in power at this period; and, as we find that Jesus was styled as the prophet, it strengthens my surmise that the prophets represented the royal leaders when in opposition. He undoubtedly led a large and well organised party, and we might conjecture, that the "Lord's Prayer" was a prayer for his restoration.

Matthew i. 1.

Under these circumstances we may be morally certain that Peter succeeded Jesus as the recognised head of the house of

Elam. It therefore follows that the present Pope Leo XIII. represents the same flag.

What a revelation is before us!

I have said enough to indicate an outline of my conception of veritable history, and leaving it to scholars for further elucidation, I will conclude in the name of the Great God, still clinging to our liturgy, still potential in its distorted form,

AMEN.

HE WHO RUNS MAY READ.

Appendix.

SACERDOTAL CHAIN ON WHICH IS FOUNDED A CLAIM OF DIVINE RIGHT TO UNIVERSAL DOMINION.

Adam	Legend.
Noah	Legend.
Abraham	Cushite Emperor.
Moses	Cushite Emperor.
David	Cushite Emperor.
Jesus	Head of the royal House of [Elam.
Peter	Head of the race of Elam.
Constantine	Emperor under the flag of Elam.
Pope Paul III.	Head of the race of Elam, who excommunicated Henry VIIIth of England for refusing to pay the Papal revenues.

The Teutonic race, probably Japhetic, throws off its allegiance to the House of Elam. This has been ingeniously characterized as a religious reformation, which cleverly obscures a momentous racial revolution.

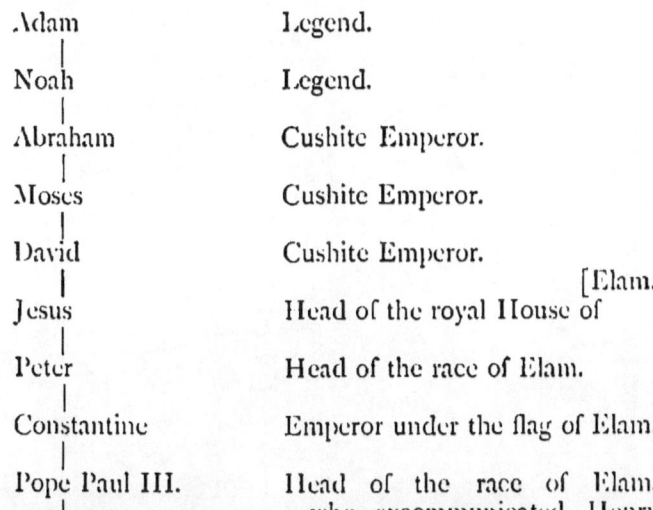

English Church still paying homage to Jesus the symbol of Papal dominion.

Roman Church

LEO XIII.
Present Pope, claiming dominion, by Divine right, over the races of Shem, Ham, and Japheth.

[*Copyright Reserved*]

LONDON;
NICHOLS AND SONS, PRINTERS, 25, PARLIAMENT STREET, WESTMINSTER.

www.ingramcontent.com/pod-product-compliance
Lightning Source LLC
Chambersburg PA
CBHW021352230426
43666CB00006B/495